Which Came First... Addiction or Disease?

By Marylyn Clark, Ph.D.

Granite Dells Publications
Prescott, Arizona

Although the author has exhaustively researched all sources to ensure the accuracy and completeness of the information contained in this book, she assumes no responsibility for errors, inaccuracies, omissions, or any other inconsistency herein. Any slights against people or organizations are unintentional.

ISBN # 1-893780-00-7

Library of Congress Cataloging in Publication Data

Library of Congress Catalog Card Number: 99-09462

Dedication

To

Mom & Dad
Paul
Steve and Ed

...and to all those who shared their lives with me
and to all who read and benefit from the words that follow.

Acknowledgments

Over the years, there were many who encouraged me to publish my work. I never felt a sense of completion. What I envisioned had not been met until now.

Without the help and encouragement of my husband Paul, I doubt whether this would have become a reality.

There have been so many people who touched my life along the way with their gifts of wisdom and love. I feel so much appreciation for all of them.

I am greatly indebted to Denton Roberts, M. Div. I gathered much knowledge from his wisdom. I am also grateful for the exposure to his friend and colleague, Robert Phillips, M.D., who filled me with the questions almost twenty years ago. All these paths crossed again during the time of this writing, which was surely not a coincidence. It began with a lost monograph, "Structural Symbiotic Systems," which was important to this work. It was one of the stepping stones along my journey.

To all those clinicians, writers, and educators who stimulated me enough to want to continue, I am indebted.

All of life is a learning opportunity and experience. Messengers of wisdom appeared before me in so many different forms—and the journey began!

Preface

In *Which Came First...*, I have attempted to raise the following questions:
- Does the environment and how we treat our body/mind alter the natural balance of things?
- Is genetics the culprit?
- Do both environment and genetics play roles?
- In what order do things happen?

The work that I have done is not scientific in nature. It comes of much reading, hands-on exposure to the lives of many, and trying to answer the many questions that have been raised over and over again.

Much of my direction came from seeds that were planted more than twenty years ago and were beyond my comprehension at the time. As I mentioned in the "Acknowledgments," much wisdom was planted by my longtime mentor, Denton Roberts. Little did I know that when he introduced me to Robert Phillips, M.D., how things would evolve. Through the years that followed, thoughts emerged and words escaped my mouth that left me puzzled. I did not know where these "out-of-the-blue" experiences came from. These proved to be the results of the seeds from the past. Over time they have been nourished as I was exposed to more knowledge and new experiences.

Contents

List of Illustations

CHAPTER I

*"Humans are beings who are souls
rather than bodies that have souls."*
Hebrew

Introduction

This is the recounting of the evolution of a journey of years and the culmination of experiences, studies, writings, etc. It is putting the finishing touches to what has felt like unfinished business since the completion of my master's thesis in 1980. I have chosen to write about my subject as a result of twenty-five years of direct exposure, the movement from a psychological to a medical model, to the current belief in a mind/body connection. So much of the addictive mind-set is black or white thinking, of which I have been guilty. It is exciting to have moved to the recognition of the connection between mind and body and speak to this in relation to the whole addictive process.

I find that it is quite exciting to theorize about the vast amount of possible effects in which the mind-body connection can be regarded with respect to changes in one's physical and behavioral patterns and how each can play a vital part in the alteration of one and/or the other.

Over many years of working in the mental health field, observing behavioral patterns, utilizing mental suggestions, watching the healing and/or self-destructive suggestions among the many, I have come to conclusions without looking at these outcomes from the view of the researcher. From a clinical sense and the experiences that I have had, I feel that I have been on a continual journey.

In terms of why I choose to write about this subject in

relation to my chosen medium, I believe that much is missed, misunderstood, and even though we look at addictive behaviors differently than in the 1930s, there is both a shame-based and/or abusive stance among those in the mental health field. There is also a need to recognize that although 12-Step programs have saved many lives, they are both shaming and abusive. It was hard for me to own up to this and move out of denial. The reason for this statement comes from recognition that those of us who get to the 12-Steps have more often than not come from shaming and abusive family systems. This is what we know, and since we bring who we are to the meetings, shame and abuse are, for the most part, a norm. Maybe it was just that which almost destroyed us in the beginning of time that saved us later—I don't know!

My theory of addiction rests with countless thoughts and ideas I have expressed to others. The effort was an attempt to make some sense of such an insidious act that on some level, those of us who have engaged in it can recognize it as insanity. To act out in an addictive way and have the feeling that as an individual you gave your power away to an attachment that became habitual feels like insanity. So much of what I have come to believe (and which really does make sense to me) could be what leads to the evolution of an addictive life style.

My Theory Of Addiction

In the late 1970s, I went to study with Dr. Robert Phillips and a group of fine colleagues in the Sierra-Nevada of California. It was here that the seed was planted in relation to mind/body connection. The subject matter at hand was the book *Structural Symbiotic Systems*, written by Dr. Phillips. The emphasis was from the perspective of Transactional Analysis and the psychological model. At that

2

point in time, I was very much engaged in the psychological model of addiction, which was viewed as Decision Theory.

In the mid-1980s I found myself in the midst of the medical model and the disease theory of addiction. Over the last twenty years, my personal experience, involvement with others and their experiences, and all the exposure to countless material was what created my desire to express in writing what I often hear myself say: "I wonder where that came from?" I do believe that all my sources, combined with an Infinite Energy, created much of what I believe in today.

When a fetus is just beginning to develop in utero, what happens when it becomes toxic? What would make the environment toxic for a fetus? Anything that would create trauma, whether it be an abusive relationship or an unwanted pregnancy. I plan to explore my thinking about this.

In utero is the beginning, and I believe this is the first stage of a mind-body connection.

So often at the time of conception, if the woman has not had her needs met, what will result is the discounting of her wants. If a woman gives birth to a baby and she herself is needy, instead of giving to the infant, she will take from the infant. This sets up an unhealthy symbiosis.[1] If the infant is, in essence, the caretaker, it learns that its needs are not important, therefore rendering them harder to identify over time. I believe that this dynamic sets up what I call *primal deprivation*. In *primal deprivation*, children come to believe, on some level, that they are not worthy or deserving of having their wants and/or needs met. They learn early that to take care of and attempt to please others is what is important. I believe that this is a setup for addiction. For is not addiction a form of instant gratification with pleasure-seeking the goal? Does not this become the way to seek to dissociate or disconnect from feelings or dealings with others?

Looking at the dynamics in the family of origin has always been important. What I am dealing with here, strictly speaking, is exploring the mental aspect of what may lead to addiction. I believe that Gerald May, M.D.,[2] in *Addiction and Grace,* put it well when he talked about an attachment becoming habituated and eventually leading to addiction. When there has been an early "narcissistic injury," I believe that the wound is great and may lead to attachments to fill the emptiness. These attachments may take many forms.

Psychological View of Addiction

Looking at addiction from a psychological viewpoint has us thinking about the perspective of a Decision Theory. If we believe this, we certainly could think of a cure from whatever it is to which we have found ourselves addicted. If this is truly a decision that we can make, then we can reverse the decision. The Decision Theory belief system would then suggest that this decision can be construed as a moral issue. There are those who believe that based on a pure Psychological Model, individuals can move from addiction to cure and settle into moderation. In other words, they assume a "take charge" attitude about how they handle the problem or issue that sent them out of control of their behavior. The behaviorists may believe that through modification of behavior we can reach a point of resolution. In the Psychological Model, we talk of an obsession of the mind.

Medical Model of Addiction

When looking at addiction as a disease, the theory that years of abuse and/or dependence has created tolerance and withdrawal and over time is progressive in nature looks different from the Psychological Model. The theory is that there are early, middle, and late stages of disease, with an acute and a chronic phase. We believe that an individual is not responsible for the disease, but once diagnosed, responsibility lies with taking the necessary steps to keep the symptoms of this disease in remission. In the medical model, this can be thought of as an "allergy of the body."

Mind/Body Model of Addiction

Here one might attempt to analyze "which came first, the chicken or the egg?" So often, clients want to explore the why and how of addiction in the early stages of recovery.

Client speaks: "Somehow, if I can clearly understand what happened and make sense of the senseless, I have the feeling that on some level I can be more accepting of my behavior, lack of control, and the insanity that I pursued without any rhyme or reason."

I do not think which comes first really matters at first. In the beginning, the important first step is to stop the abusive, irrational behavior; to put into place the necessary tools needed; to remain abstinent; and to become steady on one's feet. This is a journey, process, or path in which one must become grounded. Without any concrete facts, my intelligent guess is that "the egg" precedes. There is the question of whether there exists a genetic component to substance abuse and addiction. If there are, in fact, inherited factors, what are they?

The role of learning is an important contributing force. We do know that drugs of abuse alter the brain's normal balance and level of biochemical activity, e.g., mimicking the actions of neurotransmitters, blocking neurotransmitter action, or altering normal chemical actions that mediate transmission of information within the brain (elevating or depressing brain activity). Drugs used on a long term basis can cause permanent brain alterations and can take an unknown amount of time to reverse. So what may begin as a pleasure/reward goal of action can, in fact, alter the cellular activity of one's body. When looking at whether there are

5

inherited factors, what surfaces is the high incidence of substance abuse that seems to coexist with psychiatric conditions, e.g., Antisocial Personality Disorder (ASPD), depression, anxiety disorders, manic-depression, and schizophrenia. But, the fact still remains that no matter how high the risk, addiction requires exposure. In some cases of addiction, I believe that initial exposure may play a large part in what happens. In my own case experiences, there have been those clients who have no idea that something is wrong, who become exposed to a drug or drugs and discover that they feel better. This has been the beginning of self-medicating for many who suffer from affective disorders and/or some chemical imbalance in their bodies.

The Addictive Process

In my day-to-day practice, the link between the mind and the body and the significance that the link plays on the process of addiction become evident to me.

While working with survivors of Child Abuse Trauma, I had become increasingly aware of learned abuse methodology, which seems to become pathological. The child comes from an environment of abuse, which appears to become the norm. "This is what is familiar." The question I ask is: "Does one become attached to this abusive environment?" This is my core belief. Attachment to the abuse or crisis life-style moves to habituation that eventually results in the addiction. "The big people were abusive." From that the child "in the adult" learns how to get the same feelings through self-abuse. When the individual's need for self-abuse is not fulfilled as well as expected, he/she looks to others to help with this pattern of abuse. The child within shows others how to do that for him/her, if others do not initiate the process themselves. On the self-destructive path, an individual can use both substance and/or process addictions.

It is said that a child has in place its concept of self by the age of six. The foundation is laid by the child's perception of what is going on in its world. This is perceived as accurate, no matter how functional/dysfunctional the family system presents itself. If a child comes from extreme systems dysfunction, is the abuse the core of the altering of the mind and the shift in the body chemistry? I know the powerful position the mind plays and the emotional pain that results, and I can not help but believe that this plays a powerful physiological role on the entire body.

Theory Of Adrenaline: "Urge To Take Chances"

Is it anxiety, stress, excitement? What is that feeling that many of us would identify if we talked to someone about it before we did something to stifle the "dis-ease?" I have read that addiction is an anxiety disorder. If an individual is raised in an environment that runs on a continuum from low levels of tension to an extreme crisis levels, what goes on internally might resemble "fight or flight." There are those who have had a background of crisis in the primary support system and who have adapted to this life-style. In other words, this adoption has become the norm. Without a level of crisis, there is discomfort. There then exists a drive to recreate the familiar feeling. What I have recognized in this type of individual is that there exists the black or white edge of extreme. The rush is created and either numbed through some type of suppression or enhanced through some type of "living on the edge" activity. Those two extremes are fed from the same central point (anxiety, stress, excitement).

I became aware of this phenomenon of the creation of a crisis mode in my own personal experience more than twenty years ago. The feeling of the tension, stress, and anxiety about the project I was working on and the aware-

7

ness made me begin to feel as though my nerve endings were going to burst through the surface of my skin. What an awful feeling! I futilely searched my home for something to stop the feelings. The result was that I did something physical, e.g., washed my car, walked the dog, and did some breathing exercises. At that time, I described what I felt as an "abundance of unused energy." I shared this feeling with my eating disorder clients, and many had experienced similar events in their lives. In retrospect, I now believe that it was an overwhelming rush of adrenaline that sent me into a crisis mode. At the time, I was not consciously using any addictive behavior to numb or enhance my feelings. The crisis "junkie" has a need for chaos to produce an adrenaline rush. This form of abuse is needed because it feels so uncomfortable to be in a state of calm.

Primal Deprivation: "Running On Empty"

The subject of *primal deprivation* is very close to my heart. I do believe that much of what becomes an abusive/destructive life position has its origin there. One writer, Colman, spoke of this as "narcissistic injury." It does not matter what one calls this void or emptiness, it is just that in inner-child work, we talk about the emptiness being the "loss of the inner-child," and in some circles it is thought of as "spiritual bankruptcy."

Manifestations of *primal deprivation* are exhibited by clients in the "here and now" may be seen in the binge-purge cycle of bulimia, in the purging of money through gambling or overspending, etc. There are other examples, but these few are indicative of the setting up of the feeling of being empty/deprived. From my experience, working with all types and levels of addictions, I have frequently witnessed evidence of *primal deprivation* in clients. It appears that those who come from an environment of deprivation are invested

Figure 1.1

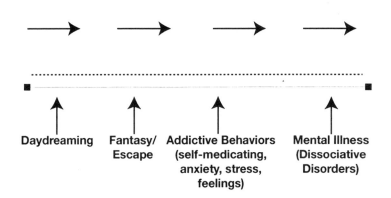

DISSOCIATION

in recreating the familiar feeling. It appears to play out as a life script or as pathological behavior.

Dissociation

The art of dissociation is a survival tool used by many as a means of escape. If I were looking at a continuum to study the degree to which one may use this, at one extreme would be recorded daydreaming and at the other extreme would be Dissociative Disorder. We all daydream from time to time, but then there are the more intense and frequent "daydreamers" who escape into a fantasy world. As we move along the continuum, we may discover that this can be an effective tool to escape from unpleasant or traumatic events. For those who are survivors of extreme dysfunction and/or traumatic events, this art of being able to dissociate becomes a means of survival. As one grows up, this method of escape may become more difficult. The common theory is that alcoholism is a form of dissociation. Those who could not dissociate well turned to substance for help. I remember the first time I heard the above statement and realized how much sense it made. I believe that many cases that move into the realm of a Dissociative Disorder may have traveled along the continuum in a progressive manner.

When "We Cease Fighting..."

These words are extrapolated from the *Text Book of Alcoholics Anonymous*. I read, studied, taught, and considered its contents as very valuable. Every time I turned a page, a new meaning might surface. I had been into 12-Steps for seven years when, just like a neon sign turned on for the first time, the *Big Book* spelled out and revealed a meaning to "we cease fighting..." that was personal. To put this meaning into words probably would bring about a response of "Big deal, I knew that!" from others—but, I finally recognized *"The Fight!"* Everything and everybody was a fight! The suppressed anger and chip on my shoulder was always there. It was what stood in the way of moving on. It was always having to be right, to control, to have the last word. To *surrender* to not having to use anger (the fight) in an abusive manner. Certainly, it created the adrenaline rush (crisis),

Figure 1.2

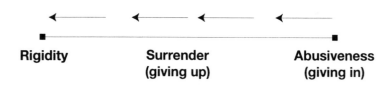

AND WE CEASE FIGHTING...

| Rigidity | Surrender (giving up) | Abusiveness (giving in) |

etc. It was truly the beginning of a liberation for me, and hopefully, in sharing my recognition with others, they will find their own true and individualized meaning.

Power Over The Will

I remember getting into a lengthy debate with someone a long time ago on the subject of "will." It was in reference to the word "willpower." At some point in time, I came to believe that although there was the word *willpower* in the dictionary, it really did not exist in the context in which it was repeatedly used. What is willpower? Well, I believe it is an attempt to have power over the will! People continually abuse themselves over not having enough willpower to stop a behavior. I remember asking a question of myself, "When will my will get out of my way?" In 12-Step programs is heard the phrase, "Self will run riot." What this suggests for me is a set up for confusion (obsession) progressing to out-of-control behavior (creating stress) that leads to compulsion. This becomes a circular cycle, since stress puts one back into a type of primal condition that promotes chemical changes in the body. Willpower, or thinking about it, sets up a feeling of—"I am in control," as opposed to "I am in charge" (which is a totally different mind/body set). Control breeds rigidity (power over will). This also can be correlated to "and we shall cease fighting anything and anyone," as a means of letting go of that control (power over will). The question of power over one's will is really about change. Letting go (surrender) seems to create a crisis due to having fear instead of faith.

"Letting Go" Versus "Crisis"

Early in my career, I remember asking a question of a respected colleague. I was frustrated because it seemed as

11

though people were coming to therapy to learn how to play their games more subtly or more efficiently, as opposed to growing or changing. The question was, "Does anyone ever really change?" The answer seemed profound to me! "Yes, once they realize it's a liberation instead of a loss." In looking at this idea with respect to my chosen subject matter, the meaning seems to have more impact. To change certainly would mean to progressively surrender to all that has encompassed one's being and to begin a reformation (rebirth).

In shifting back to addressing change from the crisis mode, the difficulty is that the energy level let the individual know that he/she was alive. It kept the inner pump creating the flow of adrenaline. The pump secreted certain chemicals that we found we needed to sedate or pump up to the edge and release what works on an individual basis. It becomes so foreign to even ponder about not being invested in creating what has become the norm, even though our paths have become both self-defeating and self-destructive. Not until an individual is willing to risk and accept that life is not working will a change of behavior be possible. Since perfection only exists in the minds of those who are controlled and rigid, my stance is that 75%-85% of the time we can act on newly-found liberation, and 15%-25% of the time the old behavior will surface. I believe that this is because perfection is not reachable. However, the good news here is that one can usually recognize the old behavior and not stay in it for long (due to change/liberation).

Addictive Population And Shame-Based Identity

Much has been written about addiction and shame. Probably the first awareness I had in relation to the powerful effect of shame was from the John Bradshaw series on the subject of alcohol and the family aired on PBS in 1980. It was not something I consciously thought about, and, in retro-spect, I can now really own the power of shame and the devastation, as it relates to *this* population. Shame plays a large part in the core belief system of countless persons. In 1971, I started working with eating disordered clients. This began a journey into the enormity of addiction and addictive behaviors. Not long after I started focusing my attention on eating disorders, I began recognizing coexisting dual addic-tions and mental disorders. These were often a complex package manifested within a single human being. I found that they were alcoholics, addicts, workaholics, gamblers, kleptomaniacs, sex addicts, etc.

Early in the '70s, I was one of the only people in Santa Barbara, California who worked with anorexia and bulimia clients. In 1985, I began work in a hospital-based chemical dependency unit. It was here that transfer of addiction started to surface over and over again. For example, in the female population, anorexia or bulimia surfaced when the treatment regimen eliminated alcohol and/or drugs "as the assumed primary addiction." In the treatment programs of the 1980s, women and men received the same treatment. The style of therapy was confrontive, shaming, and abusive. The shame-based person continued to be shamed and no one really noticed.

Fortunately, today there is a recognition among some professionals that women and men need to be treated differently to have positive results.

Which Came First...

Which came first, the chicken or the egg? This is the question asked so often in relation to addiction. Does the abuse one puts his/her body through, over time, cause the disease and/or addiction? Is it the environment, the family of origin, social exposure, genetics, or physical imperfection?

Why does this happen to some people with similar backgrounds and not to others? From my frame of reference, this does not play an important role in the solution process initially and really may not have a bearing, in the early stages. The question is: "Could it be that when there are strong indicators—people, places, things, medical conditions—current in an individual's world, is it possible that these factors may sabotage one's efforts toward freedom from addiction?" Another question asked is: "Does the abuse to our bodies throw off the chemistry?" or "Is it the genetic balance of the chemistry that creates the illness?" These questions suggest exploration of all theories or combinations that could be causal factors (physical, emotional, mental, social, spiritual).

Attachment

I believe that it is human nature to form attachments in life. If we think about it, the primal attachment commences at conception within the uterine wall and begins with an actual physical attachment to the provider via the umbilical cord, which is severed at birth. From the moment of birth, any attachments that are formed will occur externally. Throughout life, attachment formation is considered a natural process. With the norm being attachment in moderation, excessive attachment falls into a dependent/abusive category. As May (1988) cited, attachment leads to habituation, which may end in addiction. Addiction wears many faces and can cover mind, body, and feelings. Unhealthy attachments can evolve into addiction to people, places, things, substances. The tendency to attach and abuse can rise up in a single individual or be hidden until the process of recovery begins. From birth, attachment is a physical necessity. In the extreme need sense, the need to attach may flip-flop across a physical, mental, emotional, social, spiritual

14

level with a "chicken-egg" question. Recognition of the unhealthy attachment and wanting to change the dysfunctional need translates to a behavioral change which suggests loss, and with loss there could be an expectation of a grief cycle.

Exploration of obesity/emaciation as an attachment with the core issue connected to intimacy dysfunction is needed. With obesity, layers of fat create a physical boundary protecting one from intimacy. Underneath all of the insulation is the real issue of protecting the self from the "child demon" who goes out of control to feed the ego. On the surface, emaciation such as found in anorexia appears as a "don't grow up" or "don't be a woman/man!" Beneath all of the behavior is not so much fear of fat, but fear of the responsibility of being a sensual/sexual being, intimacy expectations, and fear of rejection from outside of the self. This really translates into the core "rejection of self" evolving from the obsessional perfectionistic stance that is the attachment. The attachment here is to control and feeling as though all that can be controlled is food and a distorted body image.

Structural Symbiotic Systems

What is revealed by Phillips (1975)[4], is the effects on the newborn in relation to the bonding between infant and caregiver and what the ramifications can be, based on the very core/primal relationship between the "providing system" and the "receiving system." I remember being given erroneous information that indicated the primary environment for the fetus does not have any influence on the unborn child and then discounted the importance of the foundation years. What is happening in the life of the woman who is carrying the fetus can play an important role in the health or "unhealth" of the individual. We also know the powerful and influential role of the family system in what is considered a person's life script, which may cause pathology.

Intimacy Dysfunction

There appears to be evidence of intimacy dysfunction existing with the addictive diseases. I have seen this expose itself over and over again in my work through the years. Addictions and addictive behaviors seems to run in families as some type of repetition compulsion. In the exploration of the family of origin, evidence can be found but often is disguised or even missed because the symptoms are not always exacting from generation to generation. Great-grandfather may have an affective disorder; Grandfather may be an alcoholic; Mother may have an eating disorder; and Son may be an alcoholic; and so on down the line.

The eating diseases/disorders are a good example of how intimacy dysfunction works. How one feels about his/her body often influences how closely we allow ourselves to get to others. Layers of insulation can be a boundary issue; bingeing/purging is a time consuming activity that may assist in distancing; and anorexia contributes to a slowing of the developmental process and the responsibility of relating on a mature and intimate level.

Notes

[1] Robert Phillips, M.D., wrote that a correlation can be drawn between psychophysiologic disorders with a symbiotic systems structure. The basic receiving apparatuses are those of the parent.

[2] May. Struggle to overcome attachment (addiction) involves feelings of deprivation. These feelings are painful and we must come to a place of acceptance in order to face the physical and mental struggles to be free of specific attachments.

[3] Government Notes. The theory is that substance abuse probably involves multiple genes that control various aspects of a biological response to drugs. If a genetic component were singled out, it probably would be unlikely to precipitate substance abuse and addiction. The truth of the matter is that no matter how high the vulnerability of an individual might be toward drug addiction, addiction requires exposure.

[4] Phillips. Cited above.

CHAPTER II

"...the mind resides in the body as well as the brain."
(Pert)

The field of psychology that I work in is considered a science. Insight can create movement and can be viewed as a process. I see my contributions as a possible "spoke in the wheel." As the process continues, the wheel continues to keep rolling along. I believe that anything I have put together may contribute to and/or have an element of origin elsewhere, bringing with it movement toward a deeper level of understanding. I come from a clinical background and my research is not conducted in the laboratory on rats or in test tubes. Therefore, I am never sure that what appears to be an original "discovery" has actually come before me. I can only base wisdom and discovery as mine if I have not read, heard, studied, and been aware that someone before me reached the same point or conclusion.

So many discoveries in my field evolved from interaction between client and facilitator. Other "discoveries" came from psychoeducational programs. They occurred suddenly, as though I had turned on a light bulb. Then they continued to emerge in my work with clients—other discoveries while clients participated in experiential therapy, either individually and/or groups. In my work with eating disorders, I have gained insight and then experimented with it and observed the results.

Over the past twenty-six years, I have gleaned knowledge and gathered data in my search to find answers to the many questions that have arisen on my journey. The answers evolved gradually, with one answer bringing still other questions. All I can say is that my education over the years has been many fold. I have learned so much from formal education, but there is no way that I could even compare that to what I have learned from my clients and co-workers. In the years that I worked predominantly with eating disorders (1971-1985), there were many things I explored in an effort to find some peace for those I counseled. Early in my work with anorexia nervosa, bulimia nervosa, and binge-eating disorders (then called "compulsive overeating"), I saw that there appeared to be an undertone of some sexual issues. Another clinician and I put together a questionnaire to validate my thoughts. There were twelve women in an eating disorder group. After the women filled out the questionnaire, evidence confirmed my suspicion (eleven out of the twelve had been sexually violated, and the twelfth couldn't remember). With this information, I concentrated my efforts to help individuals toward healing, with hopes that healing, along with behavioral changes, would eventually eliminate self-destructive behavior. I saw improvements, but only for a short period of time. The relapse rate was high.

I presented two case studies in a thesis prepared for my masters degree. One involved a client with anorexia and another client with bulimia. I used a host of different approaches that focused a great deal of energy on food and each individual's relationship with it. I was heavily involved with Transactional Analysis at that time, so emphasis was on Re-parenting, looking at the Script, Permission, Decision, and Re-Decision. There were many sessions that involved retraining the clients' eating behavior, and during that time, I used a Cognitive-Behavioral approach, too, presenting a great deal of education.

During these years, it also became evident that many persons were not only facing issues that involved addiction to food (eating and not eating), but also to alcohol, street drugs, prescription drugs, etc. In addition, many addicted people were suffering from anxiety, depression, and mental illness. At that time, it did not appear that there was any recognition that these symptoms created dual problems that needed to be treated concurrently.

I would like to focus on the steps that have led to the present. In 1987, something occurred to me that created a movement in another direction. This took place back about ten years ago when I designed an eating disorder program. I had been concentrating on some work one day when I became extremely uncomfortable. I felt as if all my nerve endings were going to break through my skin. As I mentioned in Chapter I, I began running through my home looking for something that would take the feeling away. I failed to find relief. I decided to wash my car and followed that with a vigorous walk with my dog. I did feel better after what seemed like an eternity. I began to believe that this had to be a buildup of unused energy. At the time, that made sense to me. I questioned clients who had eating and addiction problems and discovered that some could identify with the sensations I described. I later put together a psycho-educational lecture called, "You as an Energy System." At that point, Physical (Body) and Psychic (Mind) Energy were thought of as somewhat separate entities, one influencing the other. Looking at the deadly sins of energy loss, I emphasized that if people do not consciously direct their energies, they will be directed by their energies. This was to be interpreted as, "Whatever your attitude, it is an influential factor in what happens or how you act or react toward life in general." It seemed conclusive that what goes on in the body will affect what goes on in the mind. Here thoughts of "Which came first, the chicken or the egg," surfaced. I realized that there was no real first recognition that the human being is an energy system, a continuous energy flow (in which everything affects everything else).

I have facilitated many groups in my clinical years. In 1992, I started two, twelve week semi-structured eating disorder groups. I felt the educational component was as important as the therapeutic component. The group met for one-and a half hours with half an hour for education and one hour for process. One of the groups was designed for young adults with anorexia and/or bulimia, and the other was for adults who considered themselves to be in a dysfunctional relationship with their body and eating habits. Understanding energy was important for all to grasp—that each of us is a walking, breathing, feeling mechanism of energy. The group began to recognize that how energy is used will dictate whether a person's life-style is self-effective or defeating. Life-style, after all, is the sum total of the following: "what you are," "what you think you are, " "how you see other people," "how they see you," "what you desire to become," and "what you are doing about it?" Questions I have often asked myself were: "Are addictions just components of a complex series of diseases?" "How does anxiety fit in?" "Are addictions an attempt to deal with anxiety?" When I think of a lifetime journey that started with my own plight and the self-searching on my own behalf, the realization that the total answer does not exist alone with a clinical/psychological approach really brings to light the complexity that exists with relation to addiction, obsessive/compulsive disorder and dissociation.

In 1978, I had the opportunity to study with Robert Phillips, M.D.,[1] who had written a monograph entitled, "Structural Symbiotic Systems," which I felt contained information that was valuable. However, I was not in touch with the impact this material was to have on the evolution of my thinking in relation to the mind-body connection. The monograph used a Transactional Analysis model to express its meaning. Even if one is not familiar with basic T.A., I believe that it can be understood in its basic form. What Phillips wrote allows one to gain insight into what causes human beings to grow up in healthy ways as well as what causes pathological development.

"Symbiosis" is defined as "the intimate living together of two dissimilar organisms in a mutually beneficial relationship." As a theoretical base, a mother and a child are a symbiotic relational system. This system consists of separate organismic systems. Mother is a "providing system" and the infant/child is a "receiving system." These two systems, if they function in a healthy manner, suggest that they have a healthy organismic responses to "providing situations" and "receiving situations" throughout life.[2] This means that a "smoothly coordinated and efficient behavior emerges, involving the transfer of surplus energy to meet a personal or environmental deficit." And so the term *primal deprivation* emerged.

When I started thinking about *primal deprivation*, it was in relation to my work with eating disorders and addictions. The question I found myself asking was, "What happened, and why did it happen?" Thoughts ran through this organism called my "brain" and as these thoughts evolved, there seemed to be some relevant sense lighting my way. My theory is that when conception takes place and the fetus begins to form, this marks the beginning. The home in which the fetus nestles into, not by choice, shapes its destiny as life begins. I believe that the health of the "providing system" including mental, emotional, physical, spiritual, has a direct bearing on the "receiving system!!"

I remember attending a pops concert and listening to an obviously pregnant soprano joyously singing with an energy, sparkle, and "aliveness" that was breathtaking. Tears rolled down my cheeks as I thought about the baby nested within her. On the other hand, when I began feeling that *primal deprivation* commenced *in utero*, I realized that if the primary provider has not had her needs met in some way, or may not want the baby, or wants the baby to fulfill unmet needs, or has trauma surrounding her, etc., she will make the environment where the fetus lives become one of toxic negative energy. Phillips' theory, as I stated earlier, planted the seed, and from 1978 on, exposure to countless people, both inpatients and outpatients, and being part of a county emergency assessment team for the local hospital, resulted in pieces of the puzzle beginning to fall into place for me. My early exposure to Script Analysis (as discussed by both Eric Berne , M.D., and Claude Steiner, Ph.D., and the work of Murray Bowen , Ph.D., on family of origin issues and repetition compulsion) exemplified clearly how pathology or theme-of-life is passed down through family systems.

In 1994, a 12-Step based, facilitated program called SOAR (Survivors of Abuse in Recovery) was placed in my path. If I ever had any doubt as to HOW, WHY, and WHERE, it has been erased. While others have referred to "structural symbiotic systems," "lifescripts," "narcissistic injury," and "repetition compulsion," I continue to describe the pathology as *primal deprivation*.

When a child is born to a healthy, "providing system,"[3] it will get that which is most basic. A healthy bonding/symbiosis generated from the "providing system" to the "receiving system." When a child is born to an unhealthy "providing system," it will usually take on the role of provider. It will attempt to meet the needs of the person who may be incapable of bonding because of never having her needs met therefore creating *primary deprivation*. Since food is needed to survive along with stimulus, I believe that this lays the groundwork for a dysfunctional relationship with food and a distorted body image. The infant bonds with food and this becomes the internal and external means of stimulus. I will explore later how this sets up an addictive structure. The toxic method a mother decides she can bond with in order to nurture is the drive to meet her own needs. This results in the feeling of "primal abandonment" by the child. This pathology has the power to shift the cellular alignment of the body and set the stage for a host of mental, physical, and spiritual illnesses in later life.

If anxiety is at the core of addiction, then why not just treat the anxiety? I instruct people to tune into their daily anxieties by "journaling" about them as they surfaced. I hoped that this routine would bring about an awareness of the approximate amount of anxiety, tension, stress, and fear they were experiencing without placing emphasis on the symptom and only focusing on the cause. I could then treat the cause. The treatment that I am talking about is Thought Field Therapy.[3] I know that this treatment works! The hypothesis is that by treating the cause and continuing to shift the energy, individuals will find themselves less and less in need of that which is used to tranquillize the anxiety. One of the treatments that Roger Callahan, Ph.D., devised is called "Urge Reduction."[4] The more I thought about this treatment, the more I began to think that this could end up being a setup for failure. I thought about my years of treating eating disorders and addictions. Different clients came to my mind— people whose enthusiasm had turned to depression. Motivation and energy reached a peak, with feelings of success, and then something shifted those feelings to failure. Often this would be falling from perfection!

As a result of my thinking, I decided to make some changes in how I presented this TFT treatment. Both the treatment for anxiety/fear and urge reduction are exactly the same. Callahan[5] also believes that anxiety lies at the core of addiction. I believe that I have gone one step further in the way this treatment is presented. I will elaborate in the "Story of Kendra" when I discuss the results. Many of the therapeutic techniques used certainly were triggers that gave birth to new insights and awarenesses that opened the door to new thinking. At the same time, insight surfaced and brought with it things that were being missed and misunderstood. Some

gifts arose from the seed planted in early childhood development involving the providing/receiving relationship, the
history from one's individual prospective emerging from the
family of origin, inner-child work, toxic shame (Bradshaw),
intimacy dysfunction, boundary inadequacy, and issues of
abuse and trauma. At this point, I will focus on some case
studies that proved to be valuable and shed new light.

The names have been changed to protect the identity
of the persons involved, and in each case permission has
been granted to use information that could be valuable.

The Story Of Kendra

Kendra had been to several therapists and was a reliable
group member when I first met her in 1993. I had advertised
in a local newspaper that I was starting a Food Addiction
group. She later revealed to me that she had decided to stay
as a result of something I had said about perfectionism and
change. Since there appears to exist a black-or-white stance
or either/or philosophy among many who seem to move
toward addictive behavior, I use my own philosophy when
one addresses issues around change. I came up with a
statistic that I liked! It was not necessarily true or accurate,
but it made a point. I believe that 75-85% of the time one can
act on new behavior and 15-25% of the time one will surely
fall back into some of those old and primal behaviors (the
difference is that it will be recognized and one will not stay
there as long). Kendra was overweight. She shared that she
had bulimia (purging type) that had been arrested for about
three years. She still vacillated among binge eating, sexual
addiction, and workaholism. At the point that we began
individual and group therapy, she had distanced herself from
the opposite sex and was predominantly abusing with food
and work. This client could disassociate from her feelings
easily and appeared very much out of touch. The minute her

feelings surfaced, she could only go so far. She was able to shut down with an impish smile in order to cut the "dis-ease" (discomfort) that began to surface. I tried all kinds of different approaches with her, e.g., guided imagery, hypnosis, inner-child work, affirmations using a background of Baroque music, cognitive therapy, family of origin work, gestalt, Transactional Analysis, etc. The client would go so far then transferred back and forth with her different addictions. We did some inner-child work with a Cabbage Patch doll to represent her. The doll had a pet and she chose to have the pet represent her "imp." This proved to be very effective in her process. She was able to recognize how the "imp" came to the rescue when her feelings came up (she used the impish stance to survive early trauma). She then disassociated and detached. As far back as she could remember, tension, anxiety, and chaos (crisis) seemed the norm. At an early age, she filled her time with "doings," in order to cope. My experience of her was that of being witness to a squirrel in a cage running in circles. As she grew older, her "busy making" moved into her work, binge/purge activity, and sexual addiction. During the time I worked with her, still another addiction surfaced. Gambling became the center of her world. Between working three jobs and gambling in every free moment, her life began to fall apart. At first she won a lot of money, which of course was followed by a series of losses. She ended up with no money to buy food, pay the mortgage, or feed the dog. She found herself back to the point of having feelings of extreme deprivation. This surely was a familiar feeling.

Somewhere in my work with her, I began to realize that she kept returning to a familiar place with the original script feelings of *primal deprivation*. Feelings of peace, serenity, and success could only be temporary. Then she began the process of sabotage again. Self-defeating behaviors surfaced. When she decided to take a respite from therapy, she left her dolls behind (in case she wanted to return). She felt that with all the methods and tools she had learned, she could control her gambling and wanted to take time to assimilate all she had learned.

In May of 1996, I went for training in Thought Field Therapy (TFT)[6] and was very impressed with this powerful means of treatment. It was certainly a holistic approach. About the same time, Kendra returned to therapy. The presenting issue was intense fear of her gambling and bulimia (both meant purging and a means of creating feelings of deprivation/emptiness). She announced at this time that she would leave Arizona and move to another state in a few months. The fear of withdrawal from her addictions (work, bulimia, gambling) was overwhelming. She could no longer deny recognition of transfer of her addictions. The client was facing some major life changes: moving to another state, going from three jobs to one job, no gambling in this state, and moving in with a long distance boyfriend of many years. Both had commitment problems and had decided to give this relationship a try. As things in Arizona began to wind down, the client set a target date to stop gambling. Work was at a minimum and lots of time was suddenly available as we began the use of TFT Therapy. This client always exhibited a great deal of anxiety. One might have described her as a "spinning top," always on the move. TFT treatment for "Urge Reduction" was done on the desired target date. I had some misgivings about this treatment. Of all the treatments, this was the only one that had to be done when there was an urge. If after the treatment she still felt like acting on the urge, she was told to have or do whatever, e.g. smoke, gamble, eat. Having worked with addictions for so many years, I really felt like this was a setup for failure. Since the treatment for anxiety is essentially the same as for urge reduction, I decided to change the way I presented it to the client. I would observe the outcome over the next few weeks, hoping to reduce the anxiety and fear and with that the desire to continue the self-defeating patterns.

Baroque Music And Healing

Nancy, in her mid-fifties, was referred to me by a friend. She had suffered from serious depression for many years. Included in the many treatments were hospitalizations, shock treatment, and many changes in medications. When she appeared in my office, she presented with depression, had a flat "affect," and a very low opinion of herself. With the exception of her job as a nurse in a physician's office, she was unmotivated and felt isolated most of the time. Our goal was to somehow get her to feel better about herself and to get off Ambien (a sleep medication), which she had taken daily for more than two years.

In the beginning, the therapeutic modality was eclectic in nature. After several months of therapy, I decided to experiment with the use of affirmations differently than I had done in the past with others. I had heard that physician's were using music in the operating room during surgical procedures. Reports indicated that remarkable healing and recovery was taking place as a result. Music was my background before I pursued psychotherapy. Whenever possible, I employed music. It seemed that with healing made more rapidly and the surgical procedure[7] going more smoothly, certainly an attempt to use some type of music to heal the inner wounds of the human soul was a viable tool for experimentation. Baroque music always was a favorite of mine. Music has always played a major role in my life, and I have often used music to soothe myself and my children (in and out of *utero*). I thought, "Why not!" I decided that baroque music might be appropriate. Preparation for this took time but I had a very willing subject. The whole project took months from start to finish.

My instructions to the client were as follows:

1) Make affirmations short and simple so that a five year old would be able to understand the words.

2) Present each affirmation in three different ways: first person, third person, and using the first name, e.g.,"I like me;""You like you;""Nancy likes herself."

3) Make a sixty minute tape with baroque music in the background.

4) Listen to the tape twice a day at a time of her choosing.

One of the amazing things about making this tape was that the client became aware of how her voice changed from a shaky sound and progressed to a solid, firm, powerful sound in the weeks that it was being taped. About ten minutes of her weekly session was used to make this tape until it was complete. Before making the tape, the client was to explore the internal dialogue (self-talk) as a means of discovering the negative/positive internal conversations within her. The goal was for the client to become aware of how often she is on her "case" as opposed to being on her "side" (Denton Roberts).[8] This prelude led to working on her affirmations. The outcome of this work was completely positive. The client was to be weaned from her Ambien. Instead she just stopped it and had no trouble sleeping. Improvement was continual during the time the tape was made. Once the tape was completed, the client followed through and used it twice daily. Elaboration of the results will be discussed in the next chapter.

Lara's Theme Of Secondary Gain

Lara lived with a negative belief system throughout her whole life (faulty core beliefs). Cognitively, she understood where she was and what she was doing but did not know that she could stop her behavior with a change of attitude.

Lara had become so attached to this behavior that became habituated over the years that it truly resulted in an addiction. She appeared to be very successful in her career; however, she would not give herself any credit. On some level, she did not believe this. Anytime she did not like something or it was not her way, she moved on. Success to her was marriage, family, children, and being thin. I believe that she was consciously aware that she sabotaged herself over and over again. My hunch was that the only success she could handle would have to be on an intellectual level. In this arena she could continue to keep people in a "pseudo-close" proximity without having to really risk giving and receiving any love, affection, and intimacy. When she reached a turning point in her life, reality set in—the reality that there would be no success (as she viewed it). At the same time, her contract was not renewed at her job and there now existed the risk of having to move on when she didn't want to. It was no longer her way. A grieving process set in that was beyond any she had ever experienced. At the same time, she was faced with a major life transition/crossroad. We discussed that this grieving (in a sense) was a death (loss) of a self that was an image of what she perceived was success and which had encompassed her whole being. She could see this clearly. I gave her permission not to leave town. She did have that choice because she could survive one more year on her savings. I thought if I gave her this out and if she grasped it, the realization would move her out of this help-less and hopeless stance that she had lived all her life. We discussed her family of origin, the trauma and the dysfunction that certainly had an influence on her. Chronic morbid obesity was a real battle. She tried everything but still was on a perpetual roller coaster. I relayed to her that a lifescript of helplessness had contributed to this outcome. I asked her what the payoff was for the familiar feeling?

Often physicians look at obesity and blame all of the ills

of a person on this condition. I believe that the ills are the result of a chronic toxic mind (on one's case), which is an abusive stance. What one feeds the mind (psyche) over time affects the body (resulting in shifts in cellular balance), and this is the real cause of illness and disease. This client continually searched for someone/something to fix her. Cognitively, she could grasp this concept and know what her choices were. However, it appeared that there was some "secondary gain" involved in remaining locked into self-defeating patterns. Her slow movements along a tragic lifescript appeared locked in. This case, for me, was a perfect example of what happens when patterns become locked into a personality structure. Negative energy permeates the energy field and a resistance is set up due to the preconceived notion that "nothing works," including the self. Surrender of the *self* to a self-defeating prophecy brings with it major alterations and pollutes the energy flow and cellular makeup of a human. What follows is a slow, destructive path.

Eating Disorders, Body Image, And The Sexual Connection

I always knew that there was a sexual connection (stated earlier in this section) to all of the complex versions surrounding dysfunctional relationships with the body and the fuel necessary for survival. From the time I started working with eating issues, it was obvious that sexual trauma was part of this package. This could explain the end result quite conclusively, with support from the client that my hunch made sense. So it became logical that the anorexic did not want to grow up and face the responsibility of becoming an adult; the bulimic needed male validation for her appearance; and the compulsive overeater (now called binge-eating disorder) needed to insulate herself in order to maintain a distance from others. However, it appears to be much more complex and not as straightforward as one might think. Over the years, in all the groups I did, more continued to be revealed. I observed, again and again with obese individuals that their fears came to fruition. When the body reduced, the "sexual demon" emerged. New behavior or feared behavior was the result. While bingeing put one out-of-control, when the bingeing ceased and the body began to look good, the rise in appearance obsession was followed by an out-of-control abusive/addictive style of behavior interpreted as: "If someone loves me, is attracted to me, and wants me sexually, then I must be okay." So what emerged was an out-of-control, over-involvement in appearance and often a race for sexual conquest which equated with validation.

Reflections In The Mirror

There was the case of Sybil who had discovered that her husband had an affair. She feared that if she let herself shed weight, she would pay him back out of revenge. So for years she remained obese. Then there was Sally whose weight controlled the family and their activities. If she happened to see her reflection in a window or a mirror, the whole family was herded back into the automobile and had to return home regardless of the activity that had been planned. Now, whenever she began to lose weight, she fantasized about being in a motel with another man and having a torrid affair. This woman had a sister who was a prostitute. Sally feared that she was destined to be like her sister if she were to become thin and beautiful (equated with her perception of a prostitute).

There have been countless episodes of out-of-control sexual behavior as the end result of a change of body image. It is as if a switch is turned on that creates another being that was previously unknown. Promiscuousness and men's desire for her somehow validate that she is a really beautiful,

33

sensual, sexual being who is both wanted and desired. When she (on some level) connects that this is not real and not safe, she begins to eat so she can protect herself from this vixen whom she perceives has taken over her mind, body, and spirit!

All that has been described thus far appears to be equated to Binge Eating Disorder (Bulimia-Non-Purging Type) Often the script evolves of a perceived first male rejection.

"I'm Daddy's Little Girl," but Daddy says I'm fat, ugly, stupid, clumsy, etc. In my work I have observed that bulimia seems to connect often with the first male rejection, followed by other male rejections. This rejection somehow translates as an imperfection connected to appearance. Appearance becomes the center of one's life as it moves to an obsessional level. The person continually expends energy on body image and appearance. Often this is the result of *primal deprivation*. If there existed a dysfunctional system with a needy maternal figure, as just one example, the infant comes from a place of the most basic deprivation. In time this feeling and the discounting of needs and wants sets up the program. The familiar feeling is "deprivation," so one may binge to get to the purge or on empty, which feels like what is normal.

Binge-Eating Disorder bears resemblance to what is called "Bulimia, Non-Purging Type." The act of dieting and starvation creates feelings of deprivation. Fear of relationships and their own sexuality creates the need to hide so that they can always blame appearance ("If it weren't for...") as the cause of their isolation.

Anorexia nervosa, I believe, has a great deal to do with the dynamics of the family system. In this type of family system there seems to exist a high level of expectation for performance, whether it is in education, modeling, beauty, and sports-related competitions—stardom of a sort. There is also the pressure toward perfectionism. What is often seen is a high level of rigidity and at the same time over-involvement (enmeshed family system). The child receives these messages early on. With these messages, the child is always on stage, attempting to please in order to feel loved and accepted. The responsibility is so great and is interpreted as, "The older I get, the more expectations will be placed upon me." In addition to this, the mother is overinvolved with the child. Life seems out-of-control, and the only way the anorexic feels in control is through starvation and excessive exercise. This generates a different type of attention. What father thinks is also very important. Deprivation (or feeling empty) does take place here. The anorexic keeps the feeling going through starvation and at the same time feels powerful as she exhibits control over her body. With each of these dysfunctions exists a very private (secret) relationship between the individual and the act. The individual, along with the act (on some level, it is known to the individual that this is insanity), feels powerful.

As I continue to meet my goal, which is to bring light through other people's work, my own work and thoughts (evidence has surfaced from experiential therapy as an example), the mystery of the mind-body energy flow. Emphasis will continue to be on addictions and the question: are we really *powerless*? A stance of powerless could again be mind-body? Or does powerlessness leave us with no other choice in the plight toward liberation? Does it stop us from recognizing the cause? When I say "cause," I'm not looking at the family of origin issues, but the reaction that brings about the degree of emotion (feeling), e.g. anxiety. Instead the focus is on "the allergy of the body and the obsession of the mind!" Quiet obsessions sedate the mental/emotional reactions by changing the cellular activity (alleviates tranquilizing physical, emotional, mental pain allowing dissociation from obsession).

SOAR (Survivors of Abuse in Recovery)

As previously stated, in 1994 I was introduced to a group called SOAR (Sexton).[9] SOAR is a 12-Step model open to anyone eighteen years old and older who has come from an abusive and/or a dysfunctional background. I have facilitated this group for nearly three years. It attracts people who have been in long-term sobriety who find that life is not working out for them. They report varying degrees of discomfort. In addition, there are others who have not been involved with 12-Steps but seek the help the Steps are known to provide. I have gathered much wisdom from this experience. The group is open format, and the suggestion is made to attend at least six meetings. This is a solution oriented group with the additional goal of exploring how the past is influencing the coping methodology of the present. So often when one gets close to dealing on an emotional level regression to an earlier stage of life influences one's coping stance and/or one reverts to the coping stance that was modeled in the family of origin. This modeling usually is demonstrated in alcoholic and/or dysfunctional family systems. This dynamic is so relevant to the current relationships in our lives and is the causal factor in the breakdown of communication when dealing with emotions.

This group is very structured to avoid advice giving and crosstalk. The only prerequisites to participation is: (1) to be eighteen years old or older; (2) not to be actively suicidal, homicidal, or psychotic; (3) not to be living with the abuser; (4) and not to be abusive in the group. There are the following readings: Introduction, Definition, Situation, Solution, and the 12-Steps. The facilitator is responsible for keeping the group running smoothly, in a non-abusive fashion. When the readings are completed, the actual meeting begins. Members are able to talk for about five minutes about a suggested topic or something on their minds. The facilitator will then give feedback. At this point, the meeting is open to the members of the group. An individual may state whether or not he/she wants feedback. The presenting person listens and does not respond until all feedback is completed. After receiving feedback, the individual may relate whether or not the input has been helpful. This format has been very powerful. As a result of my work with the SOAR groups, I discovered something I had not realized previously. I began to look at abuse from a more finely-tuned prospective. This will be discussed in the following chapters.

Self-Talk

In the late '70s, I was studying Transactional Analysis, Gestalt, and several other therapeutic modalities of the time with my mentor, Denton Roberts[10]. He began to address the subject of "internal dialogue," familiar to many. He talked about being on our *"side"* and on our *"case"* —two extremes on a continuum. Being on our *"side"* releases a positive energy flow, while being on our *"case"* releases a negative energy flow. Several years ago, I guess I had a flashback to this concept when I was trying to get across the fact that self-esteem is an "inside job" which originates with our "core belief system." This belief system may not be accurate, but it was born out of *my* perspective and perception. Since words are so difficult and interpretation of those words is still more complex, it is a wonder a human being can make a decision at all. This reminds me of the case of Melody.

Melody And Her Confusion

Many years ago, Melody let simple laughter shape her life. There was however, a missing piece to her puzzle that kept her very confused. Surely she thought that if she discovered what this missing piece was, it would be something awful! One night as she slept, she had a dream and when she awoke the puzzle had been resolved. This was more than thirty-five years after the happening. What was revealed was positive. For all those years prior to this dream, mental recall was overwhelmingly negative.

Melody was just three years old when the "World's Fair" came to town. Her uncle and his best friend decided to take her to the fair. As they walked down this huge street leading to the entrance to the fair, each man grasped one of Melody's arms and they began swinging her back and forth. Melody felt so special. Her uncle had just become engaged to a beautiful strawberry blonde who was tending a booth at the fair. When they arrived, both the uncle (who was preoccupied by his fiancee) and his friend (who was girl-watching) let go of her hands. Melody became aware that they were not paying any attention to her and reported feeling somewhat abandoned (neglected) after all the attention they had paid to her earlier. It could not have been too long after, that the two young men realized that Melody was not to be found. They searched in all directions. Suddenly, they became aware of the "World's Fair Band" and the music in the background. As they looked toward the stage, they saw the conductor of the band, and, "lo and behold," next to him stood this tiny three year old with her back to the audience. She was helping to conduct. As the little girl turned around, what she saw was her uncle, his friend, and his fiancee laughing. Others were pointing and laughing, too. In her eyes, she interpreted the laughter and the pointing as something bad about her—certainly something negative. This translated to her as: "They were laughing and pointing at me and there must be something wrong with me." She did not understand that the laughter was from relief and how adorable this event was to those who saw it.

As a result of this one incident, Melody formed a faulty "core belief."[11] She thought that she was not okay in some

Figure 2.1

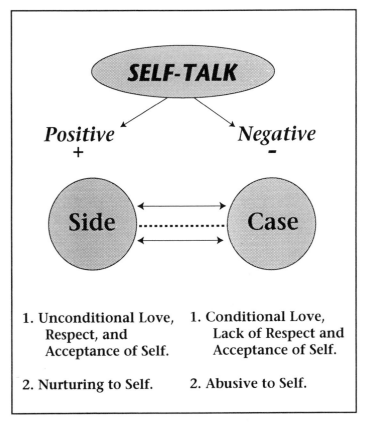

1. Unconditional Love, Respect, and Acceptance of Self.

2. Nurturing to Self.

1. Conditional Love, Lack of Respect and Acceptance of Self.

2. Abusive to Self.

way (shame-based), which resulted in her being on her "case" and discounting herself for a major portion of her life (see figure 2.1).

Self-Talk: The visual came together as a result of wanting to find a means to get those I work with to begin to realize how powerful internal dialogue is, whether positive, negative, and whether they are still caught in the web of old messages from the past. It was used to discover whether a person was discounting and into conditional love and respect (of self). Since I believe that everything affects everything else, I really support that this internal dialogue does play a part in the physical, mental, emotional, social, and spiritual health/unhealth of the individual. This followed one of my first in a series of visuals I put together as assignments for my clients. My goal was to move individuals to a place of clarity. The terminology being on your *side* or on your *case* belongs to Denton Roberts who went on to explore *Core-Beliefs*.

Obsession

To me, "obsession" is the core dynamic leading to addiction. Having worked with countless patients, I came up with an idea for a visual that I thought would be beneficial in making one aware of how obsession consumes energy. The actual idea for the visual was born out of some words I read over and over again in the *Book of Alcoholics Anonymous*. Since I am very visual, I can hear something that makes sense

Figure 2.2

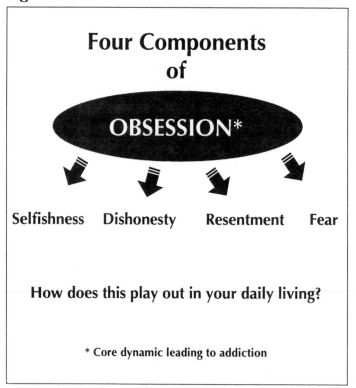

yet does not seem complete until I can have some feeling of how this looks in picture form. I devised a diagram and entitled it, "Four Components of Obsession." I wanted a patient in an inpatient treatment situation to explore this method and drew him the mental picture.

The Four Components of Obsession

Whether we speak about obsession or attachment (which is progressive), I believe we are talking about the core issue. When one moves into a place of obsession (which can become anxiety that just won't quit), the end result is some compulsive act/behavior to quiet the obsession. By exploring Selfishness, Dishonesty, Resentment, and Fear and seeing how they play out in our daily lives, we can see how obsession connects to these four areas—which in turn connects to the need for relief. Obsession results from chronic feelings of anxiety and fear. The visual was created in 1985. It proved to be a very powerful assignment for the patient for whom I created it. I have used this in my work with addictions as a means of showing rumination to be an anxiety producer that requires relief. The belief is that obsessions in some way all fall into the categories of Selfishness, Dishonesty, Resentment, and Fear. The diagram helps a person become more aware of the inner self-talk and the actions that connect. I believe that selfishness, dishonesty, resentment, and fear are the core dynamics leading to addiction. During a lifetime, a person becomes attached to certain patterns of behavior. Unless there is an awareness of this behavior, it becomes "our way" and becomes what is familiar and comfortable to us. Stop for a moment to think: *From Attachment One Moves To Habituation* (obsession)[12] *And On To Addiction* (which plays out in compulsive, driven behavior). Since the four components of obsession encompass a broad prospective under each heading, this could be an enormous undertaking. The assignment has proved to be a

Figure 2.3

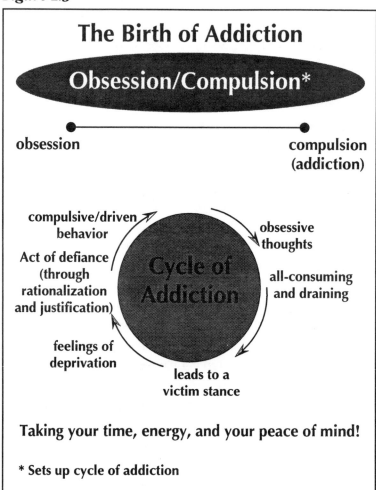

The Birth of Addiction

Obsession/Compulsion*

obsession — compulsion (addiction)

Cycle of Addiction

compulsive/driven behavior

Act of defiance (through rationalization and justification)

feelings of deprivation

obsessive thoughts

all-consuming and draining

leads to a victim stance

Taking your time, energy, and your peace of mind!

* Sets up cycle of addiction

powerful one from the very first time it was used because of a level of awareness that is usually unknown to a person.

Birth Of Addiction

This visual (Fig. 2.3) was an extension of the one on Obsession. In 1992, when I started doing a series of Eating Disorder groups, I created this as a means to further demonstrate what I feel is part of the process in the Cycle of Addiction. I feel that the diagram is simple and sends a clear message. I start with the continuum of extremes as a means of stating just that. I really believe that as the obsessive thoughts build, they become all-consuming and drain one's energy. When one is caught up in this web, it does lead to feeling like the victim. I then believe that this is compounded by feelings of deprivation which set in motion the primal feeling. This would certainly fit for the person who comes from an environment that consisted of deprivation on a primal level. The victim position often feels like deprivation and produces feelings of emptiness. I seem to always find myself looking at extremes through the medium of the continuum. I am sure that this probably evolved from a former black and white thought process. I also picture cycles as circular, in that they give the feeling of being helpless, hopeless, and trapped, with no way out. In fact, it often suggests the mouse in the maze, running in circles and trying to find an opening for the escape. For me, the birth of addiction commences with obsession and travels to the other side of the continuum toward compulsion that temporarily reduces the anxiety, stress, tension (feeling). In a step by step progression, there is movement from obsessive thoughts that lead to a victim stance. This is followed by feelings of defiance that evolve as we rationalize and justify our position. The end result is the compulsive (driven) behavior. The cycle takes time, energy, and robs one of peace of mind. For me, this is what addiction looks like cognitively (see Figure 2.3). I believe this must feel very abusive to an individual. For those who are visual and appear to have a need to have a picture of what is happening, this diagram has proven beneficial. Obsessional thoughts have the potential of setting up self-defeating and pathological behavior. I have used this diagram as part of a psychoeducational program leading to awareness. I believe that with awareness one has the opportunity to make a decision to change behaviors. Without awareness and acceptance, directional changes are not possible.

Figure 2.4

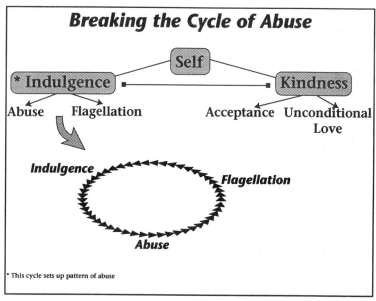

*This cycle sets up pattern of abuse

Breaking The Cycle Of Abuse

"Breaking the Cycle of Abuse" was the last of a series of self-help diagrams I put together for an Eating Disorder program I designed (1992). It was the last in the sense that until there is an awareness of what is happening, it is difficult to label the behavior as *abuse*. The continuum here is demonstrating the *self* and observing behavior from the standpoint of the two extremes, from *indulgence* at one extreme to *kindness* at the other. How often would one think of abuse as an indulgence? When a person has been accustomed throughout life to coming from a negative position (that encompasses the emptiness of deprivation and the feelings of the victim), it becomes somewhat of a norm. This type of stance is the result of the primary environment. It is natural to an individual because this is all that is known. To make changes here, one must be deliberate and have conscious awareness.

I always asked this question of the group individuals: "Do you feel that you respect yourself?" If the answer were "Yes," I would then ask, "Do you believe that you can have self-respect at the same time as when you are into self-abusing?" The answer was almost always—*"No!"* This certainly brings home a point. The problem was the fact the individual was not tuned into abuse and how subtly it can manifest itself in the behavioral patterns that have become almost ritualistic. With Self-Indulging, the movement progresses from the position of mere indulgence in the abusive thoughts, acts, and behaviors and graduates to Self-Flagellation. In order to begin to break this pattern, one must become aware of how the Indulgence begins and re-frame the Indulgence to an act of Self-Kindness, however small (see figure 2.4). Unhealthy core beliefs set up a pattern of abuse that the individual gets used to. It can almost be seen as a computer program on a screen. It probably stems from the environment of the family of origin and the perspective of the individual. This does not necessarily have to be accurate. It is however based on the individual's experience and accurate from that standpoint. As little people, we decide by the age of six who we are based on how we perceive what is going on in our world around us. See "Melody's Confusion."

Cycle Of Abuse: It seemed important at the time to enhance the meaning of Self-Talk and attempt to crawl within the individual as a means of exploring the suspected internal dynamics which keep the cycle alive. This went one step further with the continuum of movement describing the road to solution. As I thought out the visual, I began with the continuum. The continuum (for me) is representative of extremes, since the population I am addressing seldom thinks in terms of moderation, the middle or the gray. On the continuum, I placed the Self as the center point between the two extremes. Anytime a person indulges in negative self-talk (being on his/her "Case") and obsession, it becomes abusive.

The more time and energy spent in this activity, the more extreme the abuse becomes. I see the position as circular and cyclic with movement from Indulgence to Abuse to Flagellation. When I first introduced the concept to one of the groups and attempted to show how important it is to begin to notice this behavior, group members were sent home and told to buy a small spiral pocket notebook. This was so that they could record the Self-Talk/Abuse. I felt that with awareness, movement to self-kindness was possible. The second step of the assignment was to concentrate on ways of converting the negative energy into positive statements of kindness as a means to the goals of Acceptance, Unconditional Love, and Respect. The exercise became a favorite. Group members could see what they were doing and somehow loved the word "self-kindness." Being kind to themselves was so foreign. I explained that the negative energy that results from self-abuse certainly feeds on itself and is progressive. How one feels about the Self is generated throughout the body-mind, and permeates every cell, thus changing the balance of energy. I always explained that change can be in effect 75-85% of the time; and 15-25% of the time when stressed, we fall into old patterns. The only difference here is that we don't linger in old places because of awareness.

Power Over The Will/Powerless

One of the difficult and confusing discussions evolves around power, powerlessness, and willpower. People talk about having willpower and then losing it. In the 12-Step programs, the word "powerless" brings with it many comments and considerable confusion. Some see the word "powerless" as an excuse for the out-of-control behavior. "I have heard it said that I'm powerless, so it really isn't my fault." This certainly was not the intended meaning of Step One of the programs. The fact is that many individuals have a problem with the word "powerless." They interpret it as, "I told you I really am a victim." The step says "powerless over alcohol, drugs, food, etc." Many have taken this to mean "I'm powerless over everything." When I talk about "willpower," I have a hard time with that word. I turn it around to read power over my will! I have taught over the years that what I am trying to do when I'm trying to get off of a cycle of abusive/out-of-control behavior is to enforce power over my will. The battle is with my will (which is the child part of my personality). I can only enforce this power (control) over my will for limited periods of time. The reason for this is that it brings me back to deprivation and feelings of victimization with their rigid control and perfectionism. From that usually evolves "self-will-run-riot" (out-of-control behavior). This sets up stress/anxiety that is seen as a form of regression. This stress shifts the chemical balance in the body, shifting the person to out-of-control behavior to tranquilize the pain. I believe that looking at willpower is a set up for control and rigidity (power over will). I correlate this with a phrase out of the *Big Book Of Alcoholics Anonymous*, "cease fighting anything and anyone—even alcohol" as a means of letting go of the control. I like to think of being in charge of my life as opposed to being in control. I demonstrate how "being in charge" is an Open System while "being in control" is a Closed System. An individual can feel the difference on a physiological level by becoming aware of what happens in the body as these words are said. This also happens with the words "Yes" or "No," or "I hope" or "I want." It may only be semantics or the vowels used in the particular set of words. It can be considered coincidental, but it really does not matter. What matters is the impact it has had on so many people I have exposed to this way of thinking. Then, moving the thought to the experience is most influential.

Experiential Therapy

I was first exposed to Experiential Therapy in my training in Gestalt Therapy. I loved using it in conjunction with Transactional Analysis. I have used all these techniques throughout the years, when appropriate. In 1995, I decided to do a strictly Experiential Therapy group for twelve weeks. The clients involved in this setting were comprised of people who had reached some type of impasse in their process. The exercises dealt with relationships, intimacy issues, medicators (behavioral and/or chemical), self-esteem, boundaries, and included was some guided imagery. Experiential work appeared to move the individual's process toward recovery.

In the chapters to follow, I plan to pull together all of what I have written and validate the importance of my work.

Notes

[1] Robert Phillips, M.D. "Whereas the primary symbiosis is descriptively a relationship between a solidly balanced *providing* system and a *receiving* system, the secondary symbiosis is a tenously balanced relationship between a discounting system—Mother, and a grandiose system—Child." Providing behavior is, in psychoanalytic terms, seen as alloplastic adaption (the process of distribution and formation of psychic energy in the environment), whereas the receiving behavior is an autoplastic adaption (the process of distribution of psychic energy within the organism). Examples are given of the psychological symptoms that present themselves as Mother resorts to a "discounting system," and the Child meets stress in the role of the "grandiose system." Essentially, the characteristics of the hysterical depressive position are represented by the "discounting parent system" and the characteristics of the compulsive-paranoid position are represented by "the grandiose child system." The premise is "that functional psychopathology can be understood from the perspective of unhealthy symbiosis."

[2] Robert Phillips, M.D. "I assume that any organismic adaption identified as pathological, whether it be temporary or characteristic, is derived from a combination of situational environmental influences and a personal decision made at both the cognitive and affective levels." It is the nature of all systems to live as long as there is energy flow and exchange As with any system, the symbiotic systems are threatened if one member refuses or is unable to give or receive. Phillips believes that by thinking clearly and by taking appropriate action, a human organism can maintain a healthy balance between his environment (outside) and his physiology (inside).

[3] Applied kinesiology deals with the way the body's electrical energy (meridians-regular flows of electricity)

affects the well-being of the physical body. Applied kinesiology can correct bodily dysfunctions by working on these meridians. "When a meridian becomes blocked, illness or pain may result." When one does rhythmic tapping on a point on the meridian, improvement may be seen. The energy flow along that meridian seems free to move again.

[4] In one of his books, Dr. Callahan addresses the subject of food addiction. He started his work with a phobic (irrational anxiety at the core). A food addict, when anxious, has the irresistible urge to eat (seeks food for relief of anxiety). "All addictions are caused by anxiety." Connecting food with an addiction has really been overlooked much of the time. Callahan discovered the treatment for food addiction by tapping along the stomach meridian. Imbalance in the electrical system causes anxiety and sets up the breeding ground for self-sabotage. The goal with these techniques is to treat the anxiety that is at the core and causes the compulsion and food cravings. It is the energy system in the body that responds to the physical and/or mental stress. The goal of the treatment is to eliminate the anxiety. When this is done, there will not be a necessary outlet used to sedate nor a transfer of addiction.

Anxiety can be caused by an imbalance in the body's energy system, and can drive a person to his/her addiction, e.g., food. If the source of the imbalance is removed, the need to search for the tranquilizer (food, alcohol)) is not an issue.

The treatment called the "Callahan Techniques" (or "Thought Field Therapy"), works by balancing and realigning the energy system of the body. Anxiety leads to compulsive eating. The electrical circuitry goes out of alignment in some people. The cause may be internal or external and leads to anxiety. Anxiety is at the core of addictions, including food. The food and other substance and/or process addictions are used as tranquilizers.

"Anxiety is caused by specific imbalances in the body's energy system."

[5] "Thought Field Therapy" is the study of the structure of thought fields and the body's energy system as it pertains to the diagnosis and treatment of psychological problems. The most basic cause is called a "perturbation" (container of active information).

The existing hypothesis for TFT exhibits that the "body energy system is the control for the negative emotions."

"Perturbations in the thought field are the fundamental causal basis for biochemical, hormonal, neurological, and cognitive levels entailed in negative emotions." This theoretical formulation is based in the understanding in modern physics that complex energy fields and their interrelationships are the basis for all matter, including that of the human organism. The theory is that stimulation of specific points along the meridian energy system "transduces the physical energy into a form of electromagnetic energy, which has a direct and positive impact on the thought field."

In 1979, Dr. Callahan became aware of structures called "'perturbations' in the bioenergy thought field that show a precise causal relationship to psychological disorders."

[6] There is evidence of the beneficial effect of music on surgical patients. Some of the research revealed the following: changes in skin conductance, pulse rate, and blood pressure. All responses that were associated with stress were dramatically lower with the physician's choice of music and somewhat lower with researcher's music. The highest levels of stress were registered when no music was played at all, Music also seemed to improve surgeons' speed and accuracy.

[7] Life energy is all we've got to spend. This is truly determined by our attitudes and decisions and can be spent creatively (life is vital) or defensively (life is a burden or a chore). When we become aware that every event is an "exchange of energy," we can decide to take charge of how

we spend our energy. I believe that there is a link between our attitude (energy influencing our thought field) and the physical energy flow that leads to physiological health or unhealthiness. "Defensive energy is protective and reactive. Creative energy is proactive and venturing."

[8] Denton Roberts in *Able and Equal* speaks of the development of healthy core beliefs—that all people are capable, powerful, lovable, valuable, and equal. With these healthy core beliefs, there exists human esteem from which peace is built. It is based on how we feel and relate to ourselves and others. We are either for or against ourselves, which becomes the basis upon which we relate.

In creating an environment where healthy core beliefs can be nourished, "gentleness is the lubricant of learning." When this becomes the rule rather than the exception, a sense of well-being, both physiological and psychological, exists that results in a generally positive attitude toward life.

[9] Dan Sexton. See page 4, Chapter II. SOAR—Survivors of Abuse in Recovery.

[10] Gerald May, M.D., *Addiction and Grace.*

CHAPTER III

"Where the head is, the body goes."
(Denton Roberts)

A re addictions just components of a complex series of diseases? How does anxiety fit in? Are addictions attempts to deal with anxiety? What part does anger play? Is anger a reaction to anxiety?

What follows evolved from a host of unknown sources over the years of intense exposure to countless afflicted persons who have touched my life. When I think of a lifetime journey that started with my own plight and the individual self-searching on my own behalf, I realize that the answer does not exist solely with a clinical/psychological approach. The answer brings to light the complexity that exists with relation to Addiction, Obsessive Compulsive Disorder, Dissociation, and the rest of it! It really must begin with *"primal deprivation"* and end with it, since I consider this the *core*!

What I have been trying to offer as theory and present with evidence that exists in case files, is that by tracing individuals back to their beginnings exposes a validity provided to us from the history of the primary environment. There is a certain energy in this environment that produces the ingredients for the anxiety-tension (chaos/crisis) formula that sets up the programming for self-abuse/self-destructive patterns. With the proper formula, a series of outlets for attachment formation to quell the flow of the adrenaline (fight-flight) dynamic are made ready. The realization that there exists a stage prior to birth (*in utero*) and what may evolve if the "Provider" is unable to give to the "Receiving"[1] system is overwhelming. The infant enters into his/her worldly environment from a position of deficit. I have referred to several case studies in the previous section and will provide still more data to confirm what is necessary in an attempt to prove my point.

Early on in an internal and/or external dysfunctional environment, the commencement of a path or journey is influenced by this "environment." Addressed here is: what is a perception of "normal," from the standpoint of limited knowledge (information) to the individual? My statement is that, *"Primal deprivation arises with the role reversal between the providing and receiving systems in infancy."* Unless this deprivation is dealt with in the primary years, it appears to result in faulty coping in adulthood. This results in a drive toward familiarity of internal/external energy to produce feelings of deprivation (empty/void), and with it—anxiety. If it exists between the providing and receiving systems, this becomes a heightened area for dysfunctional behavior and the core of attachment (addiction) (see Figure 3.1 later in this chapter).

As I have looked at the complexity that exists here, I can explore it as it exists with food (nourishment), since this is one of the most basic needs. Without it we cannot survive. How one relates to it should be as "fuel for energy and survival." The lifeline between the fetus and maternal host is the first exposure. Some coding program malfunctions may leave a propensity for addiction, OCD, dissociation, etc. There is also malfunctioning in relation to "reaction," which produces "feelings." The resulting pattern is the dynamic of a familiar path on the same unhealthy route through life. Stress is about control. Strange as it may seem, the person addicted (attached) to stress must keep producing this feeling as a means of individual survival, which is a form of control. So being out-of-control to produce a familiar energy is being in control—paradoxical in nature.

Chaos/Crisis Abuse (Addiction)

In some of the readings I have researched, it has become evident that anxiety/stress does create changes in the chemical makeup of the body. Pert, Phillips, Borysenko[2], et al certainly have addressed that in their research. In the population I deal with, the concern, for me, has been the link between addictions and anxiety. The theory has been intertwined throughout the work I consider complex, to say the least. A straightforward statement is that underlying the addictive behaviors, I witness anxiety, and I understand that it is the culprit that causes the problem. However, it is not that straightforward. I will complicate it and then clarify my thinking, in an effort to make myself understood.

Theory:

(1) The primal environment is the prerequisite for what will follow (programming for life script).

(2) The early stages of the program are put into place with the existing level of (tension, stress, chaos, crisis) anxiety producing energy already available to program.

(3) The genetic linkage probably is a factor.

(4) Development over time of a familiar feeling that is uncomfortable but begins to be identified as normal.

(5) As with any physical/psychological progression, more energy is needed as time goes on.

So what started mainly as the barometer of energy in the primal family system environment begins to look very complex as time goes on. Although the internal feeling of a rise in adrenaline (fight and flight) certainly is not of comfort to an individual, it is measured as the "norm" so one does not feel comfortable without "the feeling." When one does not feel comfortable, the inclination is to search for comfort. This is often done by looking to create crisis, tension, and chaos, in order to perpetuate the familiar feeling. What I am saying is, "I believe that persons exist who become able to produce stress, chaos, tension, crisis, over any action or thought, so an activity can be put into place to eliminate "the feeling." The formula looks like this:

Formula:

Anxiety/Stress......>Release of Chemicals ......>Tranquilize = Relief with repetition after repetition. This is both cyclical and circular. It feels as if the more stress that is felt, the more that is produced—which triggers the behavior for relief and then the pattern repeats.

"Living On The Edge" Or "Life On High"

"Living on the edge" results from a rise in adrenaline, which creates the feeling of "fight–flight," or more simply, the "rush." There is no question that there exists a connection between addiction and anxiety. As I do an assessment in a clinical setting, exploring the family of origin history, there seems to be a common denominator. Early environments are described as "crisis oriented," "chaotic," "tense," etc. So it would appear that young people exposed to this type of energy would find themselves tense and anxious. These feelings are later identified as "normal" and become a way of life. As a child, one might escape into fantasy or dissociate as a means of escape (relief). Later this "dis-ease" may need some stronger measures to obtain relief, e.g., alcohol, drugs, work, gambling, hang gliding, etc. The paradox here is that the person can't stand the feeling, so they do what they can to stop it by whatever means. Then they can't stand being without the feeling for too long so they do whatever they can to recreate it. This creates a "double-bind" situation.

All this came to light recently. Arthur, a thirty-three year old married male came into treatment because of a level of anxiety/fear that became more and more disabling to him. He claims that five years ago his life changed as a result of being poisoned by some fish while eating in a restaurant and that this event had left his body in a toxic state. He has an overwhelming fear of having a heart attack or a stroke. As a result of his anxiety level, he has developed hypertension that is controlled by medication. Until I took a family history, he denied having problems with anxiety prior to the fish poisoning incident. I did trace a family history on the maternal side of the family that showed an elevated anxiety level in his mother and her sisters. It appears that the three females are all on prescribed medication. I proposed to the client that the environment he was raised in may have had some influence on him—in the way he behaves and how he places unrealistic expectations upon himself. He began to recognize some symptoms from when he was a teenager playing football. These symptoms are the same as those that are current, only now they are more intense. It becomes obvious that this man is attached to the extremes of his anxiety that create a rise in blood pressure, a rapid heartbeat, tightness in his chest, and the dry heaves. He states that at times he feels as though he is losing his mind. One avenue he has pursued was to become a paratrooper in the military. Currently, he is pursuing steer wrestling. While working with this client, a visual diagram came to me in relation to what is going on with the dynamic of adrenaline and becoming addicted to "the Rush" (see figure 3.1).

Sobriety And Anxiety

I propose that the origin of a demeanor of anxiety, stress, and tension comes from environmental conditioning (modeling) and may have some genetic link. The genetic link is questionable. I believe that stronger is the theory of learned behavior. I have had many cases of those in long term sobriety that out-of-the-blue come into treatment presenting with symptoms of Anxiety and Panic Disorder, and Obsessive Compulsive Disorder. Often in early recovery, the program replaces the primary addiction, and the 12-Step program and the members are used to tranquilize the stress. The healthier the person becomes, attempting to deal with feelings may create a higher risk for overwhelming anxiety. I feel that what started as an external stimulus (learned behavior) shifts nature (the balance of body chemistry), which is an internal alteration. This is why it is difficult for some people to express what has made them feel anxious. In addition, we must consider the abuse to which the body has been subjected, with the use of substance or attachment to a degree above any realm of moderation. The body has endured a great deal. Here genetics may be a factor in what results. Recent findings indicate that researchers have found a brain chemical that controls serotonin, which in turn controls anxiety. This may just be the beginning. Of course, the question I ask is: Could this brain chemical have been altered (thrown out of balance) with external/internal environmental programming? I know that the evidence lies in the future, and the answer is still not available today. I assume that this is possible based on what links already exist.

Adrenaline Addiction

So much of what addiction is all about bears the major dynamic (component) involving a paradox surrounding what I think of as a familiar feeling or familiar state of being. However you may want to look at it, I see the same outcome. I pondered about this with a client who was having a very difficult time. The anxiety/stress level in his life was becoming overwhelming. After assessing the client, I started putting a diagram together in my effort to make some sense out of what was happening to him. His difficulties were crippling to him and getting in the way of his functioning on a day-to-day basis. He had become abstinent from alcohol about two

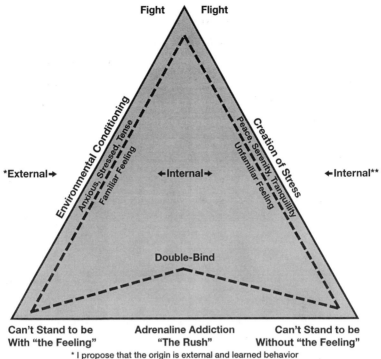

Fight | Flight

Environmental Conditioning

Anxious, Stressed, Tense
Familiar Feeling

*External→ ←Internal→ ←Internal**

Creation of Stress

Peace, Serenity, Tranquility
Unfamiliar Feeling

Double-Bind

Can't Stand to be
With "the Feeling"

Adrenaline Addiction
"The Rush"

Can't Stand to be
Without "the Feeling"

* I propose that the origin is external and learned behavior
** I propose that shifting the balance of body chemistry eventually alters nature

years prior and was currently trying to wean himself from Klonopin, which had been prescribed for him to relieve his anxiety. It took several sessions to process my thinking and to feel that the diagram was complete. It came in stages with the last insight the double-bind nature of things. What I see as having its origin in utero (external) and then continuing in the external environment after birth becomes a "familiar feeling." I propose that this feeling eventually becomes internal because of the shift in the balance of nature. If the adrenaline juices are not pumped, the individual will create the necessary stress needed to physically produce it. It becomes a double-bind situation when the individual decides to make changes and move from that familiar feeling to an unfamiliar feeling. With or without the feeling, the person is caught in the double-bind. I believe this is the core of

Transfer of Addictions and/or Relapse.

There are many who become addicted to their own body's production of adrenaline. Anxiety (the pumped up feeling) becomes the norm for these people. In Figure 3.1, what I attempted to demonstrate is that nature provides us with balance at birth. From the environmental conditioning (external) there begins the alteration of nature through learned behavior. I believe that during early programming, the conditioning is purely external. After the initial programming, the brink of the feeling is internal in nature. From time to time, there may exist an internal/external condition. Is this the point of the panic attack? In other words, the new norm (with alteration of nature) is the elevation of adrenaline exacerbated by an outside stressor. This stressor can usually be identified since it is created by some outside force. When the balance of the body chemistry is altered and we have a new norm (the pumped up feeling), even though this is uncomfortable, it also becomes uncomfortable without the feeling. So either way is uncomfortable; the only difference is that one is a familiar feeling and the other is not. This may be the factor that contributes to the "Transfer of Addictions" and the high incidence of "Relapse." I have seen this in my practice and refer to it as "sabotage." When individuals are feeling good about themselves, successful, and that life is working, is when I begin to sense the turn around (setting themselves up for failure). It manifests itself in relapse, and transfer of addictions. This can be seen in the evidence I presented in the study of Angel. My statement is that addiction to one's own adrenaline is at the root of relapse and transfer to other addictions.

You As An Energy System

It has been shown that what goes on in the mind/body affects the field of energy. It is true that the human being is

Figure 3.2

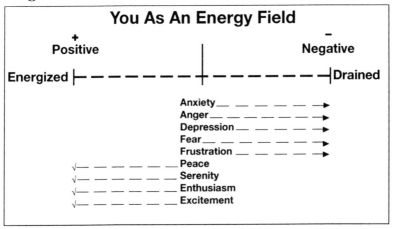

an energy system with a continuous energy flow. So we can conclude that everything a human does affects everything else in the energy system!

I have started many groups over the years. In 1992, after a respite of several years, I started two 12-week groups that were semi-structured. The educational component appeared as important as the therapeutic component. The group met for 1-1/2 hours, with 1/2 hour of education and 1 hour for process. One of the groups was for adolescents (13 to 19) with anorexia and/or bulimia; the other was for adults who considered themselves to be in a dysfunctional relationship with their body and their eating habits. Looking at energy was important to grasp. Each of us is a walking, breathing, feeling, reacting mechanism of energy. How energy is used will dictate whether a person's life-style is effective or self-defeating. Life-style, after all, is the sum total of what you are, what you think you are, how you see other people, how they see you, what you desire to become, and what you are doing about it (see Figure 3.2, "You as an Energy System").

Years ago when I studied with Denton Roberts, he talked about the power of being on your "side" and on your "case." I had started a letter to him as I was progressing with my dissertation because of a diagram that I had put together more than ten years before during the time I conducted an eating disorder group (see figure 2.1, "Self-Talk"). In 1996, I became aware for the first time of *Able and Equal* and realized that I had used Roberts' words, "on your case" and "on your side," as a means of getting clients in touch with the power of internal dialogue in relation to attitude, self-esteem, body demeanor, and, in essence, how one moves through life. The basic idea of presenting "core beliefs" came from Roberts. How I chose to use this material differs. Using this as a means of demonstrating Positive (Side), and Negative (Case) was the prerequisite to the baroque music used to accompany client affirmations. In many cases, this was the beginning of awareness at a different level.

Exploring how subtle the internal dialogue is and its impact has been enlightening. The recognition of whether a person appears to be on their case has been an eye opener. It clearly spells out whether love of self is unconditional and/or conditional, whether there is respect or non-respect, and acceptance or lack of acceptance. With all of this evolves either a nurturing or abusive stance. Of course, this is from the standpoint of black or white (either/or), which does not give a true prospective. Clients are asked to explore their individual stance with as much honesty as possible. In the clientele I work with, there is a high incidence of negativity and self-abuse. This incidence creates a more critical/judgmental attitude that certainly leads to indulging in both internal and external self-abuse. It makes perfect sense that a steady diet over years is linked to and certainly influences our attitude, which in turn affects the physical energy flow, which leads to physiological health or "unhealth." Our pattern of thinking produces psychological stress that indicates negative support in the psyche surely has an influence on the physical body. This was seen in "Lara's

Theme of Secondary Gain."

In my most recent contact with Lara, she continues to remain in her life position with an investment in self-defeating attitudes and behavior. I see little hope for her. She has always been open to all kinds of therapies and work in an attempt to move out of this tragic life script. Her follow-through is better than average for periods of time. However, it appears that rather than allowing whatever it is to infiltrate her being, her mind places an "expectation" of something that is going to fix her from the outside of her self as opposed to it being an inside job. An example of this is how a "food plan" became an "it." When she started a food plan and felt in control, everything went well. However, this would only last for a short period of time. Something would always happen (somewhat of a mind shift). Instead of just following a food plan, when "it" stopped working, she then looked at it as something that was supposed to produce a result. Her behavior was either in the form of obsession or destruction. Her obsession was with perfection and her destruction was when she fell from perfection. Then "it" did not work any longer. I attempted to explain this to her and to emphasize that to move into the gray area would provide balance or could be thought of as spiritual health (a balance of mind, body, and spirit). As I mentioned in Chapter II, I believe that a lifetime of self-defeating thoughts, attitudes, and methods pollutes the energy flow and the cellular makeup, which in time becomes fixed in the personality structure. Unfortunately, there are those who stay there. This has taken a toll on Lara—physically, mentally, emotionally, socially, and spiritually.

Deprivation/Empty/Void

I began to look at all the ways one comes back to that feeling of "empty." "Empty" is addressing what is most basic. When I think of Maslow's Hierarchy, I think about Love and

Belonging, which are primal for survival. Without food, shelter, love, and belonging there would not be survival (love and belonging is what the infant needs to fulfill stimulus hunger). The relationship between the providing/receiving systems (Phillips) is vitally important. In a healthy system, the infant has an excellent chance for a healthy journey. In an unhealthy, dysfunctional environment, there exists the setup for *primal deprivation*, leading to a discounting of wants and needs. This happens when the roles are reversed between providing and receiving. I have observed the evidence again and again in those who always return to deprivation and living on "empty." I have seen those who will go to any lengths to get there because this is their programming. A balance between the "Providing" and "Receiving" systems is imperative. When there is an imbalance, I believe that *primal deprivation* comes into play. This is especially true when there is a "role reversal." It is the setup for the discounting of needs and the losing sight of wants. This most primal exposure in the early environment (internal and external) brings with it the dynamic of "repetition compulsion"—the drive or compulsion to return to feelings of deprivation (sometimes described as "empty" or "void"). It also sets up the pattern for the ability to give or receive. To give always has a hidden agenda and to receive goes unnoticed in order to accept it. The individual does not get it because of a fear that there is a "hook" of expectation. In addition, if they were able to receive, the empty (void) feeling would be threatened. If the ability to give/receive had been balanced, then there would be the ability to give and receive for the self, which would lavish the "self" with good energy and in turn allow the free flow of this energy to others without any hidden agenda.

The Relationship Between Addictions And Anxiety

"All addictions are caused by anxiety" (Callahan)[3]. Imbalance in the body's electrical energy systems breeds anxiety. Again, this is why I place importance on the primary environment from the time of conception. Anxiety (or the foundation for it) has its early stages of development fed through the lifeline from the mother to the fetus and evolves during the first six years of life. It is directly related to the environment (external) and the reaction to the environment, physical/feeling (internal). It can be explained as an imbalance in the body's energy system that developed as a result of the external influences on the mental/physical reactions (our own individual barometer). Individual reactions are directly related to the tone of the primary environment, setting off our own emotional barometers (stances) when it comes to the end result (level of anxiety, tension, stress) measured by the impact of reaction directly related to the balance/imbalance of the family system and the environment at hand.

This leads me to the story of Kendra. Earlier it was seen that Kendra needed to create an internal environment of fear, stress, anxiety, tension to keep the adrenaline flow at a level that appeared normal for her. Her external environment was scaled to match an earlier environment that started this type of programming. Anger also could create the pumped up energy flow. Kendra was invested in being free of the internal rush which created the "dis-ease" that lead her to acting out behavior in an attempt to tranquilize herself. When I introduced her to TFT (Thought Field Therapy), the first treatment I explored with her was for *Anger*. Her daughter was getting married and she feared that her anger might ruin the wedding. Just the sight of her ex-husband would get her going, let alone the sound of his voice. The treatment was very effective. The result was that she had a wonderful time at the wedding and felt a sense of peace in relation to her former husband. When I proceeded with the treatment for *Anxiety,* I presented it differently. The treatment for *Urge Reduction* is basically the same as the one for anxiety. I had decided to work purely with anxiety. If anxiety is at the core, then I chose not to present this as anything else. I have proven countless times with many cases that this population is driven to create the anxiety in order to feel a balance in the energy system. This is paradoxical in the sense that then the goal becomes some substance or activity to take away that uncomfortable feeling. This is actually part of the makeup of the individual. So often I question what was the source of the anxiety, and the response is, "I don't know." This is where my work lies. On some level, I believe that after years of induction at this level, the cellular alteration has shifted the balance and the imbalance becomes the new balance. This is the shift that must be addressed as a means of correcting the faulty program entry and then taking on a direction to reprogram the "natural" data. The difficulty here is that the premise of TFT is a perturbation (disturbance) in the psychological energy field that creates the energy shift. When this disturbance is deliberately concentrated upon and we proceed with the treatment, the energy shifts and align-ment results.[4] The treatment for urge reduction and anxiety is the same—the only difference is what is in the thought field. In urge reduction, it is the desired substance or process as opposed to a happening as the cause of the created anxiety. In Kendra's case, I had her do the treatment when-ever she felt anxious. She reported that she would do the treatment when she began to feel her adrenaline rise, think-ing about what was happening in the moment to create the change in her internal barometer. The treatment worked. She did not have any desire to gamble, binge, or act out in any excessive/abusive activity. Kendra had bitten her nails

compulsively for years. She stopped this behavi
weeks before she noticed and reported it to me. I
that had I presented the treatment in the manner th
founder had suggested, I may not have seen the succes
I witnessed. This highly anxious and angry client finds
herself free of all the old angers, able to manage her anxiety,
with an awareness of her attachment to anxiety. The client is
confident. The knowledge that she needed the anxiety to get
the adrenaline going, that led to the relief behaviors (addictions)
to medicate, that led to the setting up of the pattern which
helped to produce self-destructive/defeating behaviors is a relief
on some level. It was certainly rewarding to connect all of this
to the toxicity in her energy field as the result and how this
destruction was circular in movement. As a clinician, it was
wonderful to observe an individual who was always "charged"
present herself with a sense of calm and balance for the first
time in the three years I had been exposed to her.

Nancy was the client whose case I presented concern-
ing the use of baroque music as a forum for the healing
process. This mode followed the exploration of her internal
dialogue (self-talk) (see Figure 2.1). It became obvious to me
that this client was predominantly "on her case." It was
important to me to make her aware of the extent of this
toxic energy that permeated her being. I did not want to
begin work with the baroque music prior to some level of
awareness being available to the client. So often this negative
energy flow is part of an automatic response to ourselves
that unless confronted and addressed, it can be said to be
"out of conscious awareness." As Nancy became more aware,
the process began with the making and use of a 60 minute
tape (affirmations with the background of baroque music).
Over the next couple of months, her entire demeanor
continued to change. She improved on a physical, mental,
emotional, social, and spiritual level. She began to assert
herself, stopped isolating, slept well, and became more

comfortable in her own skin (body). An additional reward was that she received a very high bonus at her job. Others began to be aware of the changes, too. By mutual agreement, therapy ended.

After six months, I got a call from Nancy. She stated that her life was going well but that she would like to come back and talk with me. At the first appointment, she shared her accomplishments during the time that she had not been in therapy. She also shared that she still listened to her tape (baroque music and affirmations) twice daily and that she had started a program of swimming three or four times weekly. I really believe that baroque music in conjunction with her affirmations moved her to healing and a more solid and positive sense of self. I have used the same approach with others and have seen improvement. These clients saw the improvement and were thrilled, but before long they found their way back to self-sabotaging and self-defeating behaviors. Over time there have been five or six persons who have benefited from using this method of healing.

You Are As Sick As Your Secrets

The Nelsons, Jim and Jane, [names have been changed to protect confidentiality] were a couple whom I met when they started to attend my SOAR group. After the Nelsons attended group for a period of time, they asked if they could come to see me privately for couple's counseling. Both Jim and Jane are recovering alcoholics who have been active members of AA and Alanon for many years. It appeared that they were having marital problems. In fact, they presented with communication as a big problem. Jim shared that when he and Jane first got together, they each shared, in detail, their past (childhood and much more). They both came from abusive family backgrounds. Jim shared his abandonment issues and Jane shared that one of the things that pushed her buttons was to say "no" to her in a certain way. Of course, when they decided to share, they shared all the things that make each vulnerable. Jane made a decision based on what Jim had told her that she would be the very best wife possible so that he would not ever have to suffer the way he had in the past. Jim and Jane took on the role of caretakers. With all the knowledge each had about the other, the relationship slowly became abusive. What both did not realize was that they contributed to the help needed for each to remain stuck at the emotional level of five year olds. Whenever they had to deal with each other on an emotional level, two five-year-olds attempted to communicate with each other. When each shared all with the other, they thought that they had followed the directives of the Fourth and Fifth Steps of the AA program. As time went by, Jane began to feel stifled. She attempted to reserve some part of herself for herself. She did not want to feel as if she were glued at the hip to Jim. Meetings became a way out for her. She began to attend more and more meetings, staying away from home as much as possible. During the time this was going on, Jim felt abandoned. Little by little, Jane wanted out of this relationship, while Jim hung on with every bit of energy he possessed. Through therapy, they both began to recognize how by displaying all their vulnerabilities, they had enabled the other to stay stuck in the past. Each became a party to the other's needed, accustomed level of abuse. The additional bonus each received was to "stay stuck," which did not allow for growth and solution. During therapy, we discussed methods of healing, the 12-Step program, abuse issues, etc. The concept of acceptance with relation to healing was important for each to understand. I shared with them that the way to identify healing is when the emotional connection to a particular event is gone. So many people live by the belief system that they have to continue to search for all the pieces. The result can be an addiction to this search, leaving one out of touch

Figure 3.3

Karpman Drama Triangle

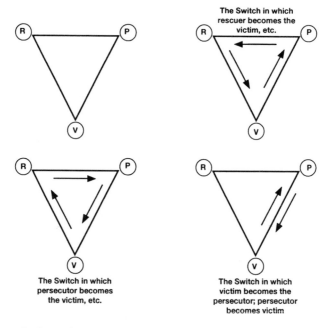

with the solution. I see acceptance as the solution. Without acceptance of the things that have happened to us in the past (which we can't change), we continue to function in the False Self System (Phillips)[5], as opposed to living a True Self System. Jim became confused through all of this. The program's Fourth and Fifth steps talk about doing a fearless inventory and then sharing it. I relayed to Jim and Jane that they shouldn't share all their vulnerabilities. Sharing in this manner can become a setup for continued abuse and staying locked into the False Self System. This led to a discussion of the teachings of the program that related to not having any secrets because, "You are as sick as your secrets." All the Fifth Step states is that you reveal this fearless moral inventory to God, yourself, and another person (not the whole world). Most of us, since we have inadequate boundaries, end up telling it to everyone. It is all in how one interprets the quotation, "You are as sick as your secrets." If one interprets it literally, I better not have any secrets! So, at meetings the members keep sharing their "war stories" over and over again, using the past as a reminder so much that the rest of the solution is lost (sobriety is only part of the solution). Jim, in his processing, did come to realize what the process is. The couple realized that they had gotten stuck in the Karpman Drama Triangle (switching between the roles of the victim, rescuer, persecutor) (see Figure 3.3) and continuing the abuse. This couple was a delight to work with because they were really open to work on fixing themselves and their relationship. This was one relationship that did not fall apart because of the past draining all the energy. I have to say it came mighty close. Jane really did want out, but called for help when Jim suggested they take a look at what was going on. Twice in the course of their therapy it appeared that they would not make it. The exciting part of this process is that they each know that they will have to work at it if they want to continue.

Even Angel Sabotages

Angel is in her mid-thirties. She is a recovering alcoholic/addict. She has transferred her addiction to anxiety, work and power (relationship/sexual addiction). I have worked with Angel on and off for several years. I met her when I conducted an aftercare program for a state clinic. After getting into trouble with the law enforcement because of her drug usage, she was given a choice of inpatient treatment or incarceration. Angel is a single-parent with four young children. After treatment, she became determined to put her life together, stay sober, get a job, and stay out of trouble. She kept to herself, taking care of her children and working as a nurse's aide. As long as she kept to herself, she did well. However, it was only a matter of time before she started setting herself up. I became aware that she was one of those who had a hard time allowing herself to have good feelings. Somehow she did not feel that she deserved to feel good about herself. One day I got a call from her stating that she was in a lot of trouble. There was a good possibility that she might face a long prison term. Angel was desperate and willing to do anything. She had gotten into trouble because of her life-style (living on the edge and always having to be pumped with an adrenaline high). In her job as a nurse's aide, she continued to take on more responsibility. She took on more jobs that involved travel away from her home base. Along with all of this busy stuff, a sex addiction began to surface. It appeared that she had a man in every port. Trouble came her way because of how she drove herself. It is truly amazing how "out-of-the-blue" crystal methamphetamine just happened her way just when she needed it. Doing too much and trying to get home when she was too sleepy and did not know how she was going to make it, she ran into someone who happened on the scene with her fix. Angel was still on probation for another offense, but thought she had nothing to worry about. Her probation officer had not bothered her for a UA for a long time. The next day she was to see her probation officer, and she was asked to have a UA at that time. Angel decided to be honest and tell him what had happened. She thought if she were honest, perhaps the consequences would not be as serious. Instead, he had her charged with possession and violation of her probation. The sad part of all of this is that she had accomplished a great deal of her goal. She had also been awarded a scholarship to nursing school, which was to start soon. Her comment to me was, "Why do I always blow it when things are going good for me?" The answer I gave her was that this is part of her pathology that started a longtime ago. She could change the outcome by changing the script and becoming willing to do whatever it took. She recognized that she continued to abuse herself with her life-style. She identified what she did to create that internal feeling needed (the adrenaline rush). Rigorous sexual activity and rigorous work were what this client identified as the ways in which she continued to be self-abusive.

Eating Disorders

So much about this complex disorder involves not wanting to grow up—not wanting to be a woman or man, not having realistic expectations, and not facing responsibilities. It is also about feelings and has nothing to do with food other than its use, lack of use, and abuse. In Chapter II, I made comment about setting the groundwork for a dysfunctional relationship with food and the body and/or body image. When food replaces other needs (leaving the infant to bond with it as an internal and external means of stimulus), there begins the basis of an attachment to meet its needs. In essence, this internal and external stimulus replaces close relationships which in time create difficulty being comfortable with intimacy and clearly defined boundaries. In fact, this stimulus becomes a relationship in itself and often leaves the individual feeling victim to its power, with intense feelings of shame. All that is desired by these kinds of individuals is for someone/something to be there to rescue and comfort them with the belief that the problem will go away. There is an unrealistic feeling that someone/something can remove this curse and make it go away. There is no connection that this is an inside job. In the case of the anorexic, the starvation (control) is a relationship, an attachment (another part of the individual). "It" has the power over the individual. I believe that this power is born of the parent and/or parents having placed so high an expectation on this individual that the lack of food intake is a statement ("If I don't eat, then I will stay small. If I am small, then there won't be as much expected of me"). The person who acts out with bulimia, with or without purging, is basically saying the same thing. The issue is about control, boundaries, intimacy, and a need not to experience feelings. Food, stuffing, purging (through vomiting, laxatives, diuretics, exercise), starving, and bingeing are all part of an attachment. Bulimia creates a very special relationship that no one can ever take away from them. I remember the first time I heard someone speak about this special relationship. They said that the relationship was theirs alone, and that they did not want to part with it. Jennie expressed this in such a vivid way. She described this part of herself (bulimia) as her "best friend." She felt safe and trusted this part and did not want to give it up. During my practice, I have heard this part of the "Self" referred to by many different names. This becomes the "Master" or the "Power" and is only known to that individual. I remember Jennie well. I tried to have her think of something else that she could form a special relationship with that would not be destructive. She did not want to consider this at all. The activity surrounding this group of complex disorders is time and energy consuming. It becomes the virtual center of the person's world, leaving little time for anything else. Everything evolves around the individual's rituals, whatever they may be. I believe that much of what goes on here is set up by anxiety, anger, obsession, shame, and originates with *primal deprivation*. This leaves the person feeling such an emptiness that only one who has been there can identify with it. There is obsession with body functions, elimination, perfection, pleasing and meeting expectations of others, and feeling so out of control—with the exception of the body.

Recently, I started working with Marla, a young college student who came to me because she questioned whether or not she had an eating disorder. In my assessment workup there appeared to be some indication of a problem in relation to food and body image. I was not sure initially, so I reserved making any diagnosis along these lines. Marla did not seem to fall into a particular slot, but there was obviously some problem. She exhibited a great deal of anxiety and fear related to achievement, perfectionism, and performance. I decided that TFT (Thought Field Therapy) might be beneficial for dealing with the issues of anxiety she was experiencing. Whatever I tried she seemed to resist. Finally, we started the treatment for anxiety. She was doing very well, when all of a sudden she began to cry. At that point, I could see a shift in her energy. When doing TFT, it is important to stay cognizant of what the problem is while doing the treatment. Midway she stopped doing the treatment. It was at this point that I noticed the shift. Marla shared that she automatically shifted from thinking of the problem when she saw an image of a bagel smothered with hummus before her, and that image replaced the problem. To me, this was a powerful insight. I realized that this was what probably happened to her when she couldn't handle anxiety, stress, fear, or tension. It did clarify for the client what she does. In another one of her later sessions, it became apparent that this client was addicted to her own thought process, which is the end result of her continual obsession. She was obsessed with perfectionism, giving herself the implied message, "If I'm not perfect, then I must be a failure." The client shared with me that she was troubled by two of her college courses. This came to light when I made another attempt to review the TFT teaching. Marla had been taught the treatment for anxiety, trauma, and grief in her sessions and had done well. She shared that it did not work for her when she tried it alone at home. During the session dealing with her perfectionism, she revealed that she had obsessional thoughts of doing the treatment perfectly (surrounding the rating of her level on a scale of 1–10). This replaced the problem she was dealing with in the thought field. In other words, she started to obsess about doing the treatment and this prevented her from following through. At the time that I became aware of what was happening, I was attempting to teach her the treatment for Obsessions /Obsessive Compulsive Disorder. I explained to her that there was no way that she could do the treatment incorrectly and that the rating scale was an abstract and not a concrete. This client is concrete in her thinking and TFT is not concrete. I continue to work with Marla at this time.

Guided Imagery

Guided imagery has proven to be a powerful source of insight in the work I have been doing with those who suffer from Eating Disorders and Body Image problems. I have several guided imagery exercises that I use. The idea for each comes from different sources and each has an unbelievable impact or outcome. This type of experiential therapy can bring up a host of buried events, creating overwhelming reactions and known only to the individual. I have clients who resist this type of experience and will not take into consideration what they may learn. It is usually these individuals who dissociate or fragment when they attempt to focus inward. They exhibit extreme fear in relation to what might be revealed as opposed to the thought that the wisdom gained could lead them one step closer to liberation

Fat Fantasy

In my years of using this imagery, clients have had many different reactions during it. The theme evolves around being at a party and slowly getting fatter and fatter and what comes up for the individual. This is followed by becoming thin and tuning into that experience. We go back and forth with the change in size. Some clients could actually get in touch with the fear that surrounded them in a thin body, such as higher expectations, competitiveness, lack of feeling safe. They identified themselves as objects, victims, as being fragile, etc. On the other side, even though there was a hatred of the fat self, her size denoted power, powerful, being noticed, being invisible, feeling safe, controlling, etc. These are just a few of the examples of feelings that were exposed during the experience. Of course, there are many more.

The Lineup[6]

This imagery deals with competitiveness. With eyes closed, each person is asked to visualize the body of each woman in the room. Each decides who has the thinnest body and who has the fattest (from an individual perspective). Next, the women are asked to form a lineup in their heads, placing the thinnest woman in the Number One spot and the fattest woman in the last spot, with everyone else in between according to where they have been placed. Then the individual must consider where she belongs in the lineup and must deal with any feelings that arise for her. After the imagery is over, chairs are set up. Each person places herself in the fat/thin continuum as seen in the imagery. If more then one person believes she should be in the same position, they are to use nonverbal means to decide who should occupy the chair. This usually brings back strong feelings about competition during childhood and adolescence. It is a powerful "letting go" exercise. This particular imagery also brings into focus the obsession to compare, which plays out in appearance obsession. There is so much body image distortion involved with this disorder.

Following this imagery, I often had butcher paper and markers available for outlining the body. Each one took turns outlining another person. This activity was followed by taping the completed outlines on the wall. Each person was allowed to see her individual outline. One of the greatest experiences happened with two anorexic-bulimics who remarked that they wished they each could have the other's body. I asked them to exchange bodies. Each one was to take the other person's outline home and study it. The assignment was to determine why the other person's body was what they wanted. The irony here was that both women were just exactly the same size except that one of them was more endowed in the rear-end. Tape measures availed each one no proof. Because of their image distortions, they could not see what was obvious. The Lineup imagery brought out a lot of internal dialogue (self-talk) and feelings each had about themselves, and how they felt they measured up in comparison to the others (Horneyak & Baker).

Beginnings

In this imagery, the client is asked to imagine that her mother is pregnant with her and is sitting at a family gathering with her father. Mother begins to daydream about the baby inside. The daydream includes the following: 1) the sex she prefers, and 2) how she wants the baby to look (color of hair, eyes, whether small or large, who the baby will look like). Father also begins to daydream about some of the same things. The imagery goes on to imagine the delivery room where the birth takes place, visualizing the mother and father (even if father is not there). It continues with imagining the birth process as the client thinks it occurred. What type of birth was it—vaginal, breech, caesarean? As the baby emerges, the doctor says, "It's a girl." What happens to father's body, expression on his face, etc. What is mother's reaction? Are the parents happy with your appearance? Then the client is to imagine mother in the recovery room daydreaming about how she would like you to look and what she would like you to be doing at your current age. The father does the same thing. When the imagery is over, there is group participation. Each person shares what they believe is mother's and then their father's ideal. The impact of this imagery brings out powerful dynamics in relation to the individual's perception of how she fits into the family system, what each parent wanted or expected, whether there was disappointment in relation to who they are and how they turned out (Horneyak & Baker).

Addictions As Seen On A Continuum—

Figure 3.4

Over Control ├────────────────┼────────────────┤ **Out of Control**

Taking Charge

What Do They Mean?

In addictive behavior what are usually seen are extremes. Anything done to extremes is considered abusive, whether we are talking about what I refer to as "over control" (which is extreme rigidity) or "out of control" (which is self-destructive). The gray area would appear to be a level of control. In my own personal view, I like to think of "taking charge" (which might just be semantics to some), but there is a different feel. When one says the words "I'm in control" out loud, there is a physiological constriction in the diaphragm.

Figure 3.5

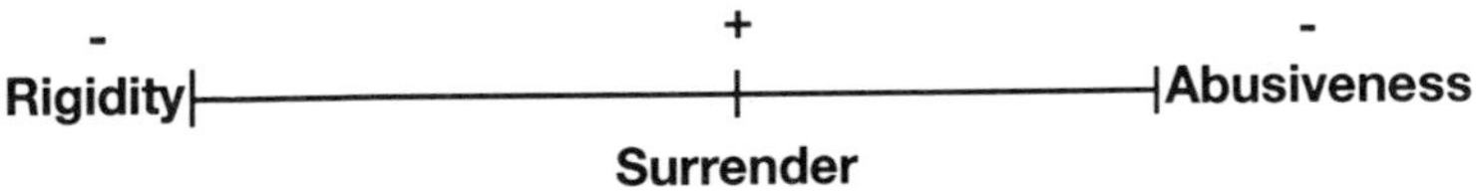

-               +   -

Rigidity ├────────────────┼────────────────┤ **Abusiveness**

Surrender

When one says, "I'm in charge," there is an open feeling in the diaphragm. An example of this occurred with Kendra when she found herself at an impasse. She wondered whether having permission to gamble would help. The question was whether this was "acting out" or "taking charge?"The next continuum emphasizes the concept of the meaning of "surrender" as it applies in the 12-Steps of AA. "To surrender" means to raise the white flag, giving up to the recognition of needing help, while "giving-in" expresses continuing the extremes of the disease/illness through a rigid or abusive stance. I will continue here using Kendra to explain this continuum. At one point her gambling felt controlled. She had given herself permission to set aside one day a week for entertainment (gambling) and designated a set sum of money to spend. During the days before the gambling session she felt "uneasy" and "rigid." She could not deal with these feelings so she went gambling and felt "relief." She described this as not feeling as if she was controlled, which led her to feeling more accepting of herself. The formula would look something like this: Rigid = Over-Control/Relief = Being in Charge.

If, in fact, the formula equates, then Acceptance of Self = Freedom =Relief = Liberation, then there might not be a follow-up of excessive behavior. If one has truly surrendered, there would not be the continued internal self-abuse. There would exist a "cease fighting!" Can we come to the gray (moderation)? Some believe so. Then can the alcoholic have a drink now and then? This was not what followed for Kendra.

Early messages of expectation from the environment (parental) to be talented, famous, a scholar, an American Beauty, doctor, lawyer, may start out with a parental dream and become distorted in the perception of the child. For the child, love is connected to pleasing and so often this molehill becomes a mountain. The child, in essence, begins to lose a sense of "self," and life becomes controlled by the inner belief that achievement of what is perceived as the parental dream is the goal. The drive is to be perfect or to please. When the discovery is made that everything seems out of control and the recognition or connection is made in relation to an area of control (food, body, gambling, spending), the feeling is very powerful. In addition, it gets a lot of attention when family members become aware. In fact, if things get bad enough, focus is diverted from the site of achievement stress. When the child loses the sense of self, obsession with feelings emerges, and there develops a progressive distorted view, slowly satisfying some secondary gain. This is the story of many young women I have seen in my practice. One case that comes to mind was of an eighteen year old, beautiful, talented young adult who was dying a slow death when I met her. She was an anorexic and a bulimic who had been starving her mind, body, and spirit since about the age of fourteen. She was an actress and a singer. Mother was a frustrated woman, struggling with a weight problem and focusing on her appearance. Father was a pilot who was a perfectionist and overly critical. This young woman felt pushed in every direction. Unfortunately, this mold is classic to so many others!

Letting Go/Surrender: "When We Cease Fighting"

The question is change and the resistance that often accompanies it. It is not that the change is difficult, it is the pain that might accompany it that becomes too much. So often people may feel as though they are letting go when there is a derailing through a crisis or some chaos to take them off track. The creation of the crisis can be considered as being on "automatic pilot." Here, the juices of addiction, the addiction to the adrenaline (rush) are used to divert themselves from the peace that might finally come with letting go. Just think about this, "When we cease fighting anything…," and how liberating that would be for the one caught up in this maze of addiction!

SOAR (Survivors Of Abuse In Recovery)[7]

As I have stated before, it was in the SOAR group that I first become aware of abuse on a very different level. I began to explore the dynamics of abuse in the addictive population and how individuals self-abuse and learn the dynamics, and if they are not abusing, well, they find enough others (in relationships) to help with the abuse. I will go one step further and state that if these individuals don't draw out someone who will help them abuse, out of conscious awareness they will educate still others how to do this. In my experience with SOAR, I discovered by the attendance of AA old timers that abuse exists within the 12-Step program. I also became aware of the abuse, control, and power that exists in some sponsors, how abusive members can be to each other, and the fashion in which one "busts the covers" of another (the confrontation). This resembles the encounter style of therapy. I found myself feeling disturbed. One of the readings in SOAR states that no one is to be abused while in group. I became aware of the misinterpretation of what it means to follow direction in the program. There is a way of following direction without being punitive. Unfortunately, in many instances the delivery becomes punitive and abusive. The very program that has saved countless lives and brought countless people to sobriety also has abusive and shaming components in it. I believe this has come about as a result of the members coming from alcoholic and dysfunctional family systems. What was modeled in the family of origin is part of the script. If the script is abusive and destructive, the individual from that background will continue in this abusive patterning. This is how it continues from generation to generation. After all, this is what was modeled and learned. What comprises the population of the meetings is what creates the cycle of abuse. In essence, the program is used to

82

hide the core of what led us to use and abuse in the first place. Could it be that a shame-based identity and a denial of the abusive stance and self-destruction is projected on to others is what helps us not to see what we don't want to see in ourselves?

One day early in my experience with this group, one of the clients I had known for more than six years began attending. He gave feedback to another male in the group. The feedback turned out to be very abusive. It was my responsibility to stop the abuse and to stop it in a non-abusive manner. It felt like a difficult chore because as this was happening, a "discovery" emerged like a bolt of lightning. It was like *deja vu.* I had heard abusive words many times before at 12-Step meetings from sponsors, friends in the program, in the old encounter groups, and, of course, in the family of origin. The words are not necessarily important. It is the type of confrontation that speaks for itself! It comes across as parental, critical, judgmental, condescending, as a put down, but in any case it has an abusive style. After the group that particular day, I continued to process this discovery. What I began to recognize was that I was aware that AA has existed since about 1935. There is not a clue as to how many people have been saved as a result of becoming a member of this community—yet the climate is abusive. It began to feel like a double-bind from the perspective of being simultaneously a lifesaving device and an abusive style environment. Now don't get me wrong; the AA program itself is not abusive! What is abusive is the behavior of the very persons who have been saved or who have saved themselves with the tools of the program! They are the perpetrators! They are the persons who fell to addiction (symptom) through their dysfunctional beginnings. They each brought with them what they learned in their primary environment (abuse, chaos, crisis, anxiety, tension, etc.). The script contin-ues and "repetition compulsion" surfaces in relationships, for they resemble the families of the past. Just as in the selection process, we often find ourselves with partners who help us recreate the family of origin so that we can produce what we may have considered our norm (whether painful or not). It was the familiarity of the past. Another discovery came into focus in relation to the selection process. There is still another way to keep the script going. If by chance we make a mistake in the "chemistry selection process" and actually meet a non-script person, I have learned that we are good teachers. This is not an act of which we are aware, but we do teach others to help us in our abuse process. It really is amazing how this happens.

The 12-Step program teaches us that "we are as sick as our secrets." How that is interpreted, I believe, is "If I want to be well, I had better refrain from having any secrets." "I don't think so!" I addressed this earlier in the case of the Nelsons.

Powerless

There are many who have a problem with the concept of being powerless. When I look at this concept from the perspective of becoming attached to something, then this makes perfect sense to me. In an attachment that becomes habituated, we progress to addiction. It is at this point that one gives up power to whatever (alcohol, drugs, food, gambling, work, sex, etc.). Whatever the attachment, it has power over the individual. In other words, until we can choose, in a sense, we are powerless over the attachment or attachments. Where the problem arises is the continuation of feeling or saying, "I am powerless," when we have let go of the attachment. I use here the disease of alcoholism, which is progressive, as an example. If we continue in recovery to look upon ourselves as powerless over certain things, the sense of powerlessness also becomes fixated into our False Self System[7]. We buy into that powerlessness and with it

there is a sense of helplessness about whatever it is that has
been our attachment—staying in the past. I think that at
some point in time in the progression of recovery and
getting in touch with the True Self System there is recognition that we have taken back our power—the power that
was once a natural part of our makeup.

Addiction To The Search

Some people become addicted to the search—always
looking for answers. I wonder whether the familiar feeling, is
again, what plays a part in this search. Peace and serenity
seem to be uncomfortable after too long. In watching people
that I work with, I have become aware of how absorbed
many are in the search. It seems to me that this is just another way of keeping crisis and chaos alive. As a result, these
people find themselves stuck, not moving toward solution or
serenity, and never having the sense that they are moving on
in their process. This is detrimental (spells out as the continuation of abuse). It does relate on some level to a need for
perfectionism. Therefore, finding one part of the puzzle leads
to looking for more pieces. This is part of living in the False
Self System (Phillips). When people come into counseling
with the presenting issue being, "We can't communicate," it
becomes evident again that communication failed because
the players involved are "acting out" of the "adapted child,"
from the dysfunctional system, or from "unhealthy core
beliefs" that we bought or that we are "acting out" of the
False Self System (Phillips). This makes sense. It will give rise
to emotions because we are often dealing from a False Self
System when on an emotional level of contact. The Search
can become just another attachment that eventually leads to
addiction, placing the individual in bondage and not allowing
movement from this position. The path continues insidiously
with the attachment of the drive to search. It is a search for

something (outside of the self) to use as a fix. This can be considered another form of Dissociation. What would happen if we would just let ourselves be? The whole idea of abuse and the drive to remember all becomes an obsession. People spend their whole lives searching, trying to bring up old memories. Memories are just that. As time passes, they become distortions of perceptions. The search, I believe, is the most subtle of the addictions. Many professionals continue to enable this process because they too believe that in order to complete the work, one must investigate and explore all avenues to put the puzzle of "why" together. It is still running on empty. The Search is to find the meaning of WHY and the meaning to LIFE! However, this combination does not allow for answers. If we think we have found one answer, it is never enough. We then continue looking for another answer. When it appears that we have the WHY solved, then can we be HEALED? If we are healed, it appears that we surely should be able to go on with life. Somehow it does not go that way, for there is always "more syrup left in the bottle." In other words, it is never empty. Even if we think we have all the pieces, the WHY does not "fix us." I believe the fixing comes with an attitude and a change in our most basic "core beliefs." As behavior and attitude shift, so will the soul begin the process of allowing for the evolution of change occurring on the way. This process is painful (not the actual change) and it is the pain that we run from, not the change. It is the pain that gives birth to the "attachments" in an effort to fix the pain. In psychoanalysis, one can "free associate" forever and continue the process over a lifetime. Phillips talks of the "human animal in and out of therapy," suggesting a never ending process. I feel the process can be an intense one for a period of time, on an individual and as-needed basis, with life and living occurring on the way. What I see so often is a holding of one's breath on the way to the "final answer" and that (the complete answer) does not really exist. There are so many components to WHY and WHAT included in the makeup of the individual. Although psychology is considered a science, it is not exacting. We still talk about theories of addiction even with all the advances that have occurred to date, so I will put my own theory into that place, which surely incorporates other theories.

Labeling Versus Identity

This subject came to mind when an old timer in the 12-Step program shared how tired she was of introducing herself as " My name is…, and I am an Alcoholic, Addict, Bulimic, etc." She went on to say that this was who she had become, in other words, who she felt she was. The SOAR group made her realize that this was another way that she continues to abuse herself—with the "Label." When one joins the 12-Step program, labeling is an important factor. There is so much denial and the introduction is a powerful way to finally come to recognize that the problem exists. To introduce oneself in this manner in the beginning, I believe, is appropriate at that time. However, when we begin to look at the progression of recovery, there comes a point in time that this kind of thinking shifts to being abusive. The shaming energy is an attachment and keeps the body out of balance. It keeps a person attached to a shame-based frame of reference. Somewhere along the line, I become my "Eating Disorder." There is no denying that I had a dysfunctional relationship with food, but I would hope that the denial is lifted in the process of recovery. If one continues to believe that they *are* the label, there is always that flow of negative energy. My feeling is that there needs to be a positive flow of energy to continue the process of recovery. I don't see this happening. Before my own personal involvement in the 12-Step programs, I had a specific reaction to people in the program. I felt that they lived in a 12' x 12' square and lived in fear of stepping out. If they stepped out, then all would be lost. I moved from that place when I began to recognize that there were those who lived graciously and peacefully with the acceptance that they chose not do drink or use. The more I am involved in this area, the more aware I am of the chains that are still there and I have thoughts of, "Does anyone ever really change?" The answer is "Yes." I don't see change effected when I am still a slave to thinking "I am powerless!" and when I still feel that "Hello, my name is .....and I am a......" even when I have chosen to live and move my energy toward a True Self[8] and recovery. This is abusive. It is very frustrating because I believe very strongly in the 12-Step program and the fact that the program has saved many lives. I guess what I dispute is that another way of feeding the addictive process is the progression to "I am my disorder" and the continuation of the internal self-punishment, shame, and the search for freedom from that is double-binding. I believe that the freedom from all of this is available once one can look at change as a liberation instead of a loss. One is not losing anything if he/she chooses not to or thinks of it as "not an option to abuse with a substance or process." The person is instead liberating himself/herself because there exists the ability to make that choice. In other words, a person is not helpless. When an individual abuses, he or she feels helpless, hopeless, and powerless. When that individual is liberated, he or she feels a sense of freedom from the enslavement to the attachments that set up this bondage.

In the final analysis, the goal is a level of liberation from all the chains that interfere with the natural flow of energy to the mind, body, and spirit!

Notes

[1] See notes in Chapter II.

[2] Borysenko, Pert, Moyers. A primary focus is conditioning, which is a powerful bridge between mind and body. Our conditioning goes a long way back. The way we react is directly related from past to present, so there is an importance to awareness as a means of unlearning attitudes that are no longer appropriate or useful. For example, a stance of chronic helplessness "depletes the brain of the vital neurotransmitter norepinephrine. This brain chemical is necessary for feelings of happiness and contentment."

Mind Traps: People destroy their self-esteem with distorted images of their bodies. Extremes of a negative view of the body can result in bulimia, anorexia, or even death. Having the negative attitude that you will never be good enough can corrode one's self-esteem.

Pert believes "...that the mind resides in the body as well as the brain." For example, anger is both mental and physical. There is what appears to be a bridge between mental and physical. Your mind is in every cell of your body. Emotions are stored in the body. They may actually be the links between mind and body. It is the body and the brain reaction that creates emotion (the body's physiological functions, both normal and pathological). Emotions have a nonphysical as well as a physical reality. Everything that you do is governed by your emotions. Intelligence is in every cell of the brain and body. The mind is more than the brain, and the brain is our view to the outside of the body (through eyes, ears, nose, mouth).

Emotional fluctuations and status do exert a direct influence on an organism, which has the possibility of getting sick or remaining well. There is a physical, biological ground for the effect of emotions on health. This has led to the theory that the chemicals that control our body and brain are the same chemicals that are involved in our emotions. This suggests theories about the "role of emotions and emotional suppression in disease, and that we'd better pay more attention to emotions with respect to health."

Emotions are the trigger of the fight-or-flight response. In a fight-or flight state, we get an adrenaline rush, our pupils dilate, and our heart starts to race. It is obvious that with the recognition of a mind-body connection, it is imperative that close attention must be paid to the whole person. This means the feelings and perceptions, how an individual views his/her health, disease, and the status of his/her illness.

The mind and body are one and the same (inseparable components of the whole). "So when one states that we can learn to use the mind to influence the body, the implication here is a dualism that does not exist."

[3] Callahan states the following: (1) all addictions are addictions to tranquilizers—all addicts are attracted to an activity or substance that tranquillizes their anxiety; (2) Anxiety is caused by an imbalance in the body's electrical (or energy) system. So if the energy system shifts out of balance, the result is a rise in anxiety. Treating anxiety with Thought Field Therapy (TFT) will eliminate use of tranquilizers of choice; (3) Addictions are difficult to treat because the people who treat them don't deal with the anxiety itself. "Addictions are the most difficult of problems to conquer." With Thought Field Therapy, the cause is treated as opposed to just the symptom!

[4] In Recovery of the True Self, Robert Phillips, M.D., explains his thoughtful approach to psychological theory and develops a holistic understanding of the dynamics of the human animal. Phillips uses the word "therapy" to signify "healing power." He states that the most important "...healing powers are those inside the sufferer, inherent to the human animal. Foremost among these powers are the processes of wound healing and the activities of the immune system."

"The are other component behaviors which are simultaneously expressed in body movement (extension and/or flexion) and physiology (adrenergic and/or cholinergic flow)." These are the natural effects (emotional components). They are natural signals—for example, the fight-or flight response. Now, in the True Self System they are just what they are. In the False Self System those biological events are judged, labeled, and manipulated" as "emotions" or "feelings."

Since the human vacillates throughout life by living simultaneously in healthy and unhealthy environments (wounding and healing), it is assumed that a natural state of health exists between cycles of predictable injury and reliable recovery. "Health and unhealth of the animal apart from the environment is a myth. It is no so much the right numbers, as it is the 'right' relationship with the environment."

⁵ Steven Karpman, Drama Triangle

⁶ Horneyak and Baker, Lineup/Beginning

⁷ Dan Sexton, SOAR

⁸ Phillips. "People are biological animals also, and each one arrives with a built-in , genetically-coded instinctual program."

Phillips proposes that "addictions are prominent alternatives in the False Self System." Characteristic of this type of individual is conspicuous consumption, and being insatiable and wasteful. We see the qualitative addictions (e.g. overeating and obesity, overimbibing and alcoholism, money-making and money spending) and qualitative deviations (e.g., drugs, gambling, vehicular speeding, sexual athleticism, sadomasochistic energy transfers), which stunt any reciprocal enrichment provided by nature and people. The human animal seeks pleasure and tries to avoid pain. Addictions appear to begin pleasurably and temporarily do anesthetize against pain.

The steps before addiction are attachment and then habituation (which can provide comfort), which can eventually lead to addiction. "Affect (emotion) is the basic energy of life for the human animal." Affect in the False Self System is abused, and to extort benefits it is manipulated to control others. In the True Self System, which is naturally healthy, children are able to express feelings (sadness, anger, joy, fear), and they are honored.

Children take on special roles in the family or origin for survival. Whether healthy or unhealthy, it is most natural that under stress the human animal will return to the primary survival patterns, which may include self-defeating behavior. When Phillips indicates that perhaps even in utero the infant is wounded by the energy between the parents in the event that they do not want the pregnancy.

When parents have low self-esteem or are demoralized or embittered, there is a strong propensity for role reversal between parent and child (ren). The child, in essence, takes on the parental role (which interrupts the natural development of the child and establishes chronic patterns of dysfunction). When there is a healthy family system, the parents are predominantly in a Providing role, with the children in a Receiving role. Parent and child are also in the opposite role when appropriate. Now, here lies the culprit within the role reversal in that the healthy occasional providing by the child and receiving by the parent is also reversed. This becomes a great burden to the mind and body of the developing child.

[9] Phillips. Becoming aware of and telling one's truth is usually healing and is necessary for the recovery and maintenance of health. Change is difficult. The goal toward recovery of the True Self includes and involves psychological, physiological, physical, spiritual, and social pains inherent to psychotherapy. "Interpersonal relationships in the False Self Systems are characterized by the infliction and acceptance of some degree of abuse." This is also true with respect to the

individual's relationship in the workplace, civic and religious organizations, and with government and culture at large. When one is able to say, "I am now willing to take the scary step of giving and receiving only abuse-free love," one is ready to replace the False Self System with True Self direction. Phillips states, "…to not forgive is to not let go of abuse," and "…to not forgive is to remain frozen in time." Genuine forgiveness does involve anxiety, pain, sadness, and anger for the forgiver and the forgiven.

Often, as adults, when we are finally able to ward off abuse and mistreatment, we are willing to settle for that because we are in a slightly better position. After all, caretaking seasoned with abuse is part of the expected norm. We get to where most of us are unwilling to let go of the hurtful pleasures of negative communication. It seems difficult to give up companionships that shower us with a mixture of nurture and abuse.

"If the holistic perspective is true, as I believe, then everything is connected to everything for the human animal." Truism involves a person's biological, psychological, and spiritual systems. It also applies to the concentric environment of society, culture, and nature.

All categories of psychological illness are results of living life from the False Self System (these are the symptoms). The unique themes that psychotherapists often see in the current life of patients were conditioned by the particular circumstances of early life in the family of origin. These themes recur in personal relationships, work life, and dream life.

CHAPTER IV

"An image may or may not represent external reality,
but always represents internal reality."
Martin L. Rossman, M.D.

In this chapter, I will discuss how I feel my findings could affect society as a whole. This can actually take place if those who are engaged professionally in this field of study begin to look at the impact of the points I address. I hope for some recognition that provides validation or just the desire on the part of professionals to explore the possible authenticity of what I am proposing. This, for me, would be an important movement in the right direction. I will attempt to show the progression of my thinking along the lines of this designated format of exposure.

There were many ways I went about expounding on the points I was addressing. At times it might have appeared as if I had taken off in still another direction—when all it actually was is my style of writing, expressing, and possibly showing still another road that brought me back to the same point. I may just want to show still another aspect of what I see. In the end, the goal/purpose is to open up the channels to comprehend addictive behaviors at a deeper level and a deeper meaning to what I say when I refer to a "holistic approach to treatment" (although many would argue that we are following along a continuum of a holistic approach). It is only on some level that this is true. I want to know that when I work with a human being, I consider both the internal and external environments and their influences on human energy, with its realities and outcomes. I believe that I have shown that the way one lives life, thinks, and acts contributes to and is a major factor in the chemistry or the chemical makeup of the entire system. Until recently (7-8 years), I used a "tunnel vision" method of treatment. I see many colleagues who are still where they were when they started in the field. There exists the rigidity of what is characteristic to black and white thinking (one way or no way). In order to give a picture of what I see and have seen, I went about this with a "pick and shovel," sifting out any information I thought might shed light, and with it tear down the walls built with rigid cement. In my introduction, I explored Theories of Addiction, The Addictive Process, and many areas that I believe emerged during the process. I have translated my own meaning to several areas of concern in the consideration of this complex dilemma/issue. I do like the word "dilemma" or "issue" as opposed to "disorder." It does work for me! "Disorder" somehow comes across as some awful thing I have and with it goes a whopping amount of power! I soften some presentations as a means of not giving something more power than I choose. In all that I explore, what I show is the complexity of the addictions, how I believe they evolve, how the chemistry of the body is altered (making it extremely difficult to emerge from the maze). With the alteration of balance, transcends the transfer of addiction. It would seem as if there were no hope. This is where therapy and alternative healing methods come into play. Everything affects everything else in the human energy system! Within the human being is a field of energy that flows through the systems. I will focus on the literary works that represent the areas of study that seemed important as a point of validation, along and in conjunction with my discussion. There were several important points to this study that will be clarified. The review is presented from the psychological and medical model of addictions—the mind/body and spiritual connection. What we see is that it becomes more difficult to separate these areas. Each of the literary works overlap in presentation, and not one exclusively addresses its individual medium. I see all the material presented as vital to a better understanding of addictive behaviors and the relationship these behaviors have on the energy system of the human being. It would be difficult to actually separate the psychological and medical models, since on some level each of the works presented refers to one and/or the other and the impact of each on the other. The psyche needs positive support to function well and the physical body needs to be free of psychological stress in order to function well. If there exists a negative internal dialogue (of energy), eventually the physical body is affected, causing the breakdown of healthy cells (Roberts). Even though Roberts focuses on the psyche, he addresses the impact of the core beliefs on the psyche and its effect on the body. "Core beliefs are to the psyche what organs are to the body." Roberts believes that "where the head is, the body goes." In other words, feelings are a biochemical process. A general stance of "being on my case" allows stress to accumulate in one's system and will eventually manifest itself in physical disease. Feelings are a biochemical process (Roberts). An awareness of the unhealthy core beliefs is the first step toward moving out of a stance that helps produce the toxic energy flow. "Mind is brain and brain is body." (May)[1] May talks about the importance of the natural balance and that imbalance of the system is progressive. It was May who brought me to believe that attachments are addictions and in our struggle to overcome these attachments (addictions), feelings of deprivation evolve. I stepped back with this to my thoughts on *primal deprivation*—the beginning stage for unnatural attachment making the struggle (physical and mental) more painful. I do agree that acceptance is what is needed to begin the healing process. Chemical balances determine what happens in the body. Addictions play a vital part in shifting these chemical balances. An example is tolerance in alcohol abuse and the body establishing a new chemical balance so that more and more alcohol is needed to achieve the desired effect. In order for the body to work in harmony, the natural balance must be maintained (May). One of the results is stress. If addiction is about anxiety (the core), then what May says makes sense. What I proposed in my dialogue in the presented cases certainly does support the theory of chemical imbalance as a precursor to anxiety/stress. I'm just going one step further in my description of a different order. I suggest that the origin was learned from the early environment (external stimulus), which eventually created the chemical imbalance leading to attachment, habituation, and addiction as the means for tranquilizing the learned stress (anxiety). With chronicity comes an internal shift that is produced automatically as a result of the new balance creating still another imbalance. Much of the work I have presented evolves from the material from two writings by Robert Phillips—"Structural Symbiotic Systems" and "Recovery of The True Self." The main theme of "Structural Symbiotic Systems" is the relationship between the psychophysiologic disorders from the prospective of a symbiotic systems structure (Phillips). A primary symbiosis is a relationship between a solidly balanced "Providing and Receiving System." Phillips addresses this subject from a biological view and calls the outcome "the Secondary Symbiosis that is between a discounting-system (Mother) and a grandiose-system (Child)." The aftermath of these physical ramifications is quite interesting. As I stated earlier, it was here that the seeds were planted for further exploration along these lines and I began to question how this impacts addiction. The light bulb first came on in relation to eating dysfunctions. I started to think of this closest (bonding) survival issue between mother and child. If this issue was not a healthy symbiosis, then it could be considered the most *primal deprivation*. I thought about many ways that this could happen and how it could manifest itself. As I thought about them, those I have explored in case histories in this study emerged. They seemed to tell the story according to my mind's eye, e.g., Kendra, Lara, Marla, etc. It appeared that they enjoined with food initially to produce the nurturing that was not available to them. They attached to food (survival) as a means of fulfilling a stimulus hunger. I also believe that this is the precursor to boundary inadequacy and intimacy dysfunction. Phillips states that "psychosis is understood as the failure in establishment of symbiosis" and "...character disorder is seen as a pseudo-symbiotic phenomenon (the inter-psychic outcome of two similar organisms living together in narcissism rather than mutuality." This also fits with me and has been expressed as such in the case of Lara. The result has been some secondary gain over the years that has left her locked in the personality disorder thus far. I propose that this started out as a pseudo-symbiotic phenomenon. Phillips assumed that this adaptation derived from a combination of situational environmental influences and a personal decision on a cognitive and affective level. In Figure 3.1, I draw this out as a means of expressing what I theorize happens. The onset is the result of the environment. This happens at the point when it becomes internally produced (after a time) and nature's chemistry is altered. The young person does make a decision, from her own perspective as to where she fits in (in her little world), which may not be accurate. This is at a cognitive level of the core-belief system. It is at the "core-belief" level that it moves to the affective level. This is an area in which both Roberts and Phillips say the same thing. It may appear that I, too, am expressing the same thing. The difference that I see is that I go one step further and attempt to draw a picture of what I actually think is happening. I do agree with Phillips, that by taking action, a human organism can maintain a healthy balance between environment (outside) and physiology (inside). An excessive rush produced by our brain or by internal means moves us into self-defeating behaviors and keeps that rush coming (Cruse)[2]. Cruse calls this "co-dependency." I have a problem with the use of that word. "Co-dependency" became a catchall word for all dysfunctional relationships. In fact, for a while it seemed like an excuse or a means to an end for a "cop out" to everything in relation to behavior. Everything and anything was called "co-dependent." Cruse defines co-dependency as a pattern of painful dependency on compulsive behaviors compiled while looking for approval from others that intermingles with the excessive rush produced by the brain as a result. In essence, we essentially say the same thing and just call it something different. I chose to think of this as adrenaline, crisis, chaos addiction, when one progresses to the late stages and becomes addicted to his/her own production of this chemical. This has come about because of alterations in the chemical makeup of the body. I believe that this is the key to why we transfer from one type of self-defeating behavior to another. It is all to accomplish the same internal experience with an end desire for relief. In order for the healing process to take place and a beginning made toward being in charge of one's physical and emotional well-being, it is important to gain an understanding of mind/body (Borysenko)[3]. Borysenko addresses a holistic approach toward this accomplishment. Much of the work I have done was geared toward sending that message. Without looking at the individual from every aspect, we miss the necessary links needed to bring about a process of healing. Psychoneuroimmunology (PNI)[4] goes one step further and takes into consideration the immune system that plays a part in the body's ability to defend itself because it is a path to our emotions, hopes, and fears. Our mode of reaction is formulated from the past, often producing attitudes that are destructive. Chronic helplessness depletes the brain of norepinephrine (necessary for happiness and contentment). To be aware of this depletion is important. Chronic helplessness is exemplified in Lara's case. PNI clearly defines the relationship with mind and body. Chronic stress and lack of balance contributes to illness. If we think about this in relation to the family of origin, with trauma and toxicity in the environment, surely we can see evidence of imbalance affecting the balance of a person that could have as its result some sort of substance abuse and/or addiction. Lara relayed a story to me when she visited at Christmas. She was standing at the back of the plane because she did not fit in her seat and she was miserable. There was a little boy next to her. She overheard him ask, "Mommy, why is that lady standing?" As Lara heard the boy, her internal self-talk was as follows: "I'm so fat that I don't fit in the seat, and standing up is my punishment for being a bad girl!" She refrained from saying it out loud.

Thought Field Therapy became an important addition to the work I was doing in the course of my research into addictive behaviors. It appears that it has clarified my thinking and again produced some doubt in relation to the disease model. Thought Field Therapy has me wondering again. When I look at the products of my process based on the diagrams I have devised, I get caught with the "chicken or the egg" concept again. Is it addiction or disease that came first?

Based on all I have gathered, I can honestly say that addictive behaviors can cause disease! Disease can come about as the result of chronic physical and mental abusive and destructive behavior. It is what I do and how I treat my body-mind (energy field)—not who I am that becomes the positive or negative investment in health or "unhealth." I propose that learned behavior (see figure 3.1) can cause disease as opposed to the opposite and that this is the case a large percentage of the time.[5]

In May and August of 1996, I engaged in a training program in an effort to learn Thought Field Therapy (TFT). I have to admit that I was very skeptical about the whole thing at first. I read Callahan's book, *Why Do I Eat When I'm Not Hungry,* and viewed an informative video. Each had some of the methodology available for use. I did not feel comfortable using this methodology in my practice until I had some formal training. I became a believer as a result of becoming a subject. While using this with my clients who seemed prone to addictive behaviors and transfer of addictions, I found myself excited by the results.

I had a surprise visit from Kendra on Christmas, 1996. It was great to see her. She really is a different Kendra. It was a pleasure to see a calm and serene person sitting before me. It gave me an opportunity to do some follow-up questioning. In the time she was gone, she had to use the treatment for anxiety twice and reported that it worked well. Kendra reported that there was no desire to gamble. She was comfortable with one job, did not eat compulsively, and she now enjoyed being at home. The bonus, of course, is that she was still not biting her fingernails and had long nails for the first time in her life. In addition, she related that she did go out gambling with one of her friends when she came to town and woke up the next morning with a bad hangover (does not drink or smoke). Now she really has no desire to gamble again. When she agreed to go with her friend, she did fear that she would be triggered again. It must be remembered that I did not do the classic Urge Reduction treatment in this case because I felt that this could result in a setup for failure. Kendra knows she has something available to her if she becomes anxious or obsessed with those old "learned behaviors" that drive her to her addictions.

If all addictive behaviors are caused by anxiety, is anxiety the result of the biochemical shift or a learned behavior? I believe that the biochemical shift is the result of the learned behavior. This is what I have attempted to show in my work. It would then stand to reason that the learned behavior becomes an attachment that becomes habituated and results in addiction. The addiction eventually becomes a causal factor leading to disease, e.g. cirrhosis, cancer, diabetes, etc. Callahan talks about there being an imbalance in the energy system caused by a psychological disturbance in the thought field.

Earlier I wrote that anxiety can be caused by an imbalance in the body's energy system. But is that really true? As I progressed in this work, I began to wonder whether anxiety is produced (learned) in the early environment, and, if that is so, then the imbalance in our energy field must be the resulting factor which can outlet into addiction in an attempt to bring about a sense of balance. It does not work. It becomes a temporary relief. Does anxiety throw the system out of balance? Or does the system shifting out of balance cause the anxiety? Addictions have been hard to treat because anxiety is not usually taken into account. The focus is on changing the behavior. Usually, people shift to another addiction to medicate the feeling. If a person becomes addiction free, he/she may find himself/herself incurring panic attacks, having frequent mood swings, or facing severe bouts of depression. I have encountered the extremes many times in dealing with clients during long-term sobriety.

Tom had been in recovery for more than ten years when he experienced his first panic attack while attending an AA meeting. I received an emergency phone call from him. He scheduled an appointment and returned to therapy with a sense of bewilderment about his dilemma. I referred him to his primary care physician for a medical checkup to rule out any illness. At the time I had not been exposed to TFT and resorted to the use of relaxation techniques, hypnosis, and cognitive therapy. Eventually, he was referred to a psychiatrist who prescribed Klonopin (with which Tom was uncomfortable). After a while, he was able to accept the medication and did well on it. Should he ever return to therapy he would be a perfect candidate for Thought Field Therapy for Panic Attacks.

A "perturbation" is defined as a container of active information which brings on negative emotions. "The body energy system is the control for emotions." If this statement is true, then Callahan is saying the same thing as I have been saying. The perturbation is the causal basis for negative emotions on the biochemical, hormonal, neurological, and cognitive levels. I see TFT as a valuable asset in the field of mental/physical wellness. Since addiction is symptomatic of other things, dealing with addictions from the viewpoint of "what is the cause" may be the answer to eventually eliminating the addiction. In dealing with the cause and eliminating it, Urge Reduction may not be the choice I would make. The only problem that exists in my mind at this point is addressing individuals who have become addicted to their own adrenaline and can't come up with the thought or problem to do a SUD's (Subjective Units of Distress) rating. These individuals don't know what it is that they are anxious about (the adrenaline high is produced automatically). In this type of situation, looking at the actual driven behavior as an Urge may be the only answer.

I have always related the mind and its functions to the brain. At least that is what I thought I was thinking. Mind resides in the body as well (Pert). Pert thinks about one entity of a "body-mind." If anger is both mental and physical, what about other emotions? Anxiety is a reaction to what is in the environment, with basic features that are innate and built upon from that point. Anxiety is a physiological reaction to tension, stress, and fear. Reactions are related to individual perceptions. These perceptions are related to life experience, knowledge, or lack of knowledge. Our early environments do color our perceptions, therefore tempering our reactions. They are based on the health or "unhealth" of the environment (system). The chemicals that control our brains are the same chemicals that run our bodies and are involved in our emotions. This suggests that emotions or suppression of emotions plays a role in disease. This is also effective in alcohol/drug/food abuse. If substance is used to dissociate from feelings, then these feelings are suppressed/repressed and could be a factor in the formation of diseases, evidenced along with these forms of abuse on the energy system. Obsessive Compulsive Disorder[5] is anxiety that just won't quit, and brings with it the continual drive toward ritualistic behavior in an attempt to find some relief (rituals or self-soothing devices). It is in the first four years of life (time of bonding between the mother and the child) that there is a vulnerability to OCD (Levenkron). My tendency leans toward belief that this vulnerability to anxiety or anxiety disorders, including OCD, runs along a continuum that could start as early as in utero and increases progressively during the first six years of life. The severity is directly related to the level of impairment/dysfunction in the family system. We all basically say the same thing. Phillips speaks of the initial primary symbiosis (healthy) which relates to the maternal bonding, and I speak about the origin of the foundation for anxisüy resting with "*primal deprivation*." The bonding does not occur because of the unhealthy maternal state, maternal immaturity, or the level of maternal neediness. This affects the relationship between the "providing and receiving systems" (Phillips). The question is, do the seeds for this inability to bond precede birth because of heredity? I really believe that the predisposition for this inability to bond can be passed down from generation to generation, but I lean toward it being a learned behavior and part of the modeling process. I have seen this in my practice with Gail.

Gail came to me by order of the court at age fourteen. What a pretty child she was—far too old for her biological years and exposed to more trouble than someone her age should be! In my early assessment, it became obvious that this 14 year old was the product of *primal deprivation*. She became the parent figure to her immature, helpless mother. I could safely say that the normal bonding between the two had never taken place. When Gail was fourteen, Gail's mother decided that she was going to finally take on the role of the parent. Problems mounted as she attempted to take charge. Gail continued to act out and get into trouble. She was arrested and locked up repeatedly for alcohol/drug use, shoplifting, running away, and violating her probation. I had my suspicions all along as to what may have happened here. Problems were escalating when I decided to invite mother and maternal grandmother to a session. Gail had begged for this for a long time. The mother and the grandmother showed up and we waited for Gail. She never came. We learned later that she had been arrested immediately before the time of her appointment. However, the information that was made available during this session that was to have involved the three generations was quite beneficial even without Gail. Grandmother was a lovely woman who seemed warm and cooperative. Mother was fragile, immature, and passive-aggressive. When the grandmother shared with me that she was not raised in her family of origin, lived in foster homes, married young, and was a teenage mother, things began to fall into place. She tried so hard to bond with her little girl, but she was too needy and immature herself. It was so obvious that her daughter was probably the provider and became the next needy and immature generation. It became apparent that when she had Gail, she was needy. When Gail was born, her mother was into chemical abuse, and the father also was an alcoholic/addict. Mother divorced when Gail was an infant and there were many men in her life as Gail grew up. Gail and her mother did not have a healthy symbiosis, which led to still another generation of dysfunction and deprivation and the setting of the mold again. Gail is an adrenaline addict. Living on the edge has kept her going.

She will soon turn eighteen. Until very recently, shoplifting, drugs, alcohol, sex, and getting arrested kept her adrenaline going. She is finally getting her life together after a long struggle.

In literature distributed by the U.S. Congress[7], the authors state that drugs of abuse can bring about complex action in the brain, which results in a variety of behaviors. Drug abuse interacts with the mechanisms of the brain. This is associated with neuroadaptive responses. Abusing drugs can and does alter behaviors and responses, which tells me that whatever we put in our bodies in the form of substance has the capacity to alter the body's natural order. An important statement made in the Congressional literature is that even if there were a genetic component and even if there were a high vulnerability toward drug addiction, addiction requires exposure. This is very true. Without exposure I do not believe that the addiction would just happen. This reminds me of a 73 year old woman who had never been exposed to alcohol because of the teachings of her religion. When I met her, she had lost her husband and was very depressed. She paid a visit to her physician, but because of her age, he did not want to give her tranquilizers. He told her that either a glass of wine or brandy before bed would help her to relax and she would sleep better. Since the doctor prescribed this regimen instead of medication, she followed his instruction. Within a three month period, she exhibited alcoholic behaviors and was hospitalized for treatment. She died shortly after. It appeared that she probably was vulnerable to alcohol. As long as she was not exposed to it, there was no problem. According to scientists, if there is a neurochemical dysfunction with addiction, they call it a "chemical deficiency" of dopamine and serotonin. If one believes that this is a disease, such as diabetes, it could be recognized as a "brain chemistry deficiency disease." My question again is whether this is the result of the abuse —or is the abuse a result of the disorder? Which came first?

Working in this field for so long, I have come to the conclusion that the power is in the patient. In fact, I'll go one step further and state that the healing power is in the patient. In "The Recovery of the True Self," Phillips makes reference to the word "container"[7] (uterus, mother's arms, the Ego, and the concentric environments of society and Nature—a holding, cuddling environment). More simply stated, the container is one's parental environment in infancy and one's Ego later. Callahan speaks of "container" in a different sense. He connects this word with the word "perturbation" as the container of active information. I place *primal deprivation* with the negative emotion that is generated around feelings of deprivation that provides the links that lead to anxiety and the like. It is in the inborn program (nature) that the alteration process begins when the container is in a state of disturbance. Phillips describes the human animal using a cellular model as a means of depicting the development of what he calls the "False Self System." When there is an unbalanced environment, there is an unbalanced family who in turn raise unbalanced children, creating an unbalanced family system. When I refer to deprivation, what I propose is that it results from a place (environment) of unmet needs or extreme dysfunction. Deprivation arises from the basic environmental structure available to the fetus or infant child, and this sets the stage. In the Gestalt sense, there is the "unfinished business" of the childhoods of the union that created the new life. The emotional state of the mother is important to the fetal physiology, and the development in utero is certainly influenced by family patterns, maternal physiology, and preconceived parental expectations. This is the beginning of the development of the "False Self System" or an adapted (altered) Self, based on fulfilling a role for the creators. It appears as a type of obligatory stance which sets up feelings of deprivation, with the energy expended in a caretaking role. I believe this begins the cellular alterations that create the chemical imbalances. In a physiological sense, diseases do result from ambivalent providing and receiving. Since this is not the natural state of things and makes up an individual's "False Self System," it is understandable. Again, the natural flow of energy is disturbed, throwing the chemistry off and with it ushering in the probability of physical and/or psychological disturbance. I like the use of the label "False Self System" and "True Self System" (Phillips). It makes it easier to understand what Phillips tries to say to us. I could call these two parts of the Self "Front and Back Stage," "Pretend and Real," "Negative and Positive," "Role Model and Real Model." In any case, the words "Role" and "Real" fit for me. When we start out in a dysfunctional system, and when we decide from our perspective of what is in our environment, in and out of utero, we play the "Role" we believe we're supposed to, thus altering the balance of nature and planting the early seeds of internal stress. Now, on the other hand, if our environment is healthy with those who are there and involved, with the balance in order, we can be "Real," which allows the natural development to evolve in the normal process of things. I propose that the birth of addiction comes about as a result of the "Role," and is, in fact, an alternative or a means of dissociation from the stress of being something other than ourselves. Addictions are prominent alternatives to the False Self System. So, in essence, Phillips and I are in agreement; Phillips' work does truly support my thinking. What I have noticed repeatedly with those with whom I work with in my private practice is that when a person has taken on a "Role," that "Role" is connected to an issue surrounding survival. When a person is able to be "Real," there is no stress related to survival. It indicates that the environment is healthy, safe, and balanced. I believe that whatever we call what is going on, there is a strong hold on the human being. This is why I

Figure 4.1

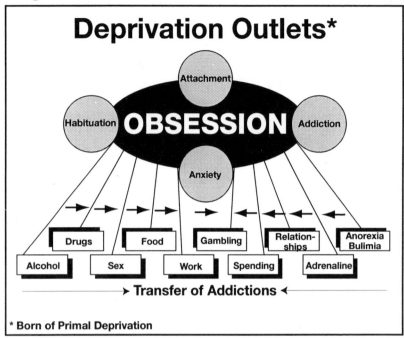

Deprivation Outlets*

Attachment

Habituation **OBSESSION** Addiction

Anxiety

| Drugs | Food | Gambling | Relation-ships | Anorexia Bulimia |
| Alcohol | Sex | Work | Spending | Adrenaline |

→ **Transfer of Addictions** ←

* Born of Primal Deprivation

state that 75% to 85% of the time we will be able to act on
new behavior. Fifteen to 25% of the time while under stress,
it is natural to return to the survival patterns that may
include self-defeating patterns. Caretaking, seasoned by
abuse, has become a part of an expected norm. It appears
difficult for us to give up relationships that offer a mixture of
nurture and abuse. This seems to be where we come to an
impasse in the nature of things.

    Primal Deprivation: What I have said over and over
again is that *primal deprivation* is at the core and what
individual pathology follows, stems from the beginning. I can
compare it on some level to not getting enough oxygen and
seeing the resulting damage to the internal mechanism of
the brain. *Primal deprivation* creates that inner void (empty
feeling). The necessary balance of stimulus that nourishes
(feeds) the mind, body, spirit and is relative to the degree
that it was lacking, is missing. *Primal Deprivation* in the

extreme sense might create a condition known as "Marasmus," in which no stimulus is available. Death would result as the spine shrivels.

Deprivation Outlets: This visual was my way of looking at the substitutions for healthy interactions, intimacy, and the ways of keeping a distance from others or relating in a superficial or pseudo-close manner. The outlet (attachment/addiction) becomes the center with the goal being to fill the void. With each of these outlets, we attempt to tranquilize ourselves and at the same time fill the void (emptiness). The end result is feelings of deprivation. These come to the surface disguised as feelings of helplessness, hopelessness, powerlessness, and with it are what is described as "empty" feelings. Some refer to this as the loss of the inner-child (which I would express as loss of what was natural) due to the family of origin dysfunction.

As a means of summing up my discussion, I will show, in some manner, how I see the bodily response and/or activity aroused by a stimulus (see Figure 4.2).

Addictive Process: Figure 4.2 was the last of the series and seemed appropriate as part of a summation. Describing this process is my way of expanding the interpretation of my thoughts through more than one type of experience. Words and pictures are complementary. Since the process is circular and cyclic, I wanted to show how I visualize the progression. Eric Berne was the founder of Transactional Analysis. He said that "all of us are born Princes or Princesses and somewhere along the way we decide that we are Frogs." None of us chooses our parents. At conception (beginnings), if there is a healthy union of sperm and egg, all will be well (for the most part) and growth will take place in a womb that has an inviting environment. The visual depicts the state of "unhealth" in the primary environment in order to address the subject at hand. I see that the shifting of natural balance commences with an energy when deprivation is in place.

Figure 4.2

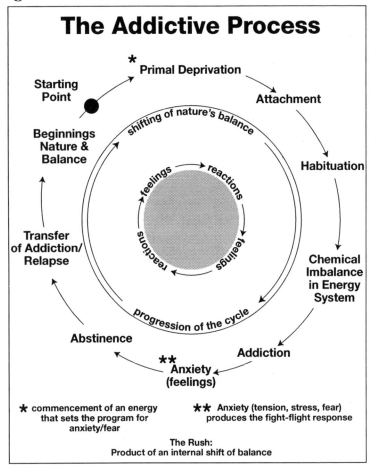

The Addictive Process

Starting Point

* **Primal Deprivation**

Attachment

Beginnings Nature & Balance

shifting of nature's balance

feelings → reactions

reactions ← feelings

Habituation

Transfer of Addiction/ Relapse

Chemical Imbalance in Energy System

progression of the cycle

Abstinence

** **Anxiety (feelings)**

Addiction

* commencement of an energy that sets the program for anxiety/fear

** Anxiety (tension, stress, fear) produces the fight-flight response

The Rush:
Product of an internal shift of balance

This balance shift proceeds with the creation of certain learned reactions and sets the barometer for feelings. Through movement an attachment to this "malaise" may be relieved with food. In essence, this is the beginning of the attachment to the familiar feeling. The next stage is habituation and with it comes the continuation of the chemical imbalance in the energy field, which in turn becomes the new balance. The reaction/feeling continues to rotate, creating stress/anxiety that just won't quit. As we get older and use substances, people, places, and things for relief, decisions to move to a condition of abstinence do come into play. This is where "dis-ease" commences, and the result may lead to a relapse or transfer of addiction. In this tangled web there are so many internal messages that feed the wheel, e.g. feelings of deprivation, shame, emptiness, helplessness, feeling undeserving, etc. All of this stresses the system that creates the toxic energy juices (rush) as we keep pedaling along (see Figure 4.1).

Body Reaction In Response To A Stimulus

Learned: This is acquired learning patterns versus innate learning patterns.

Innate: This belongs to us from birth and belongs to the our central nature.

Learned/Conditioned ——— Reaction ——— Innate

Since a reaction is a bodily response to or an activity aroused by a stimulus, the question is how much of this is learned from early environmental conditioning and how much of it is innate? If there are responses that belong to an individual from birth, are they the outcome of the experience in utero? When we look at genetics and heredity and see certain abnormal propensities in family systems (carried down from one generation to another), questions always arise. Is it learned or are the genes, cells, internal mechanisms defective? There are so many questions, and when they are answered, there are more questions that come from the answers. I would love to have concrete answers available. If I were the biologist or the scientist, I would be able to validate some or all of what I have proposed.

Notes

[1]Gerald May, M.D. wrote that the mind plays a vital role in the process of addiction (one might think of this as a mind trick), for example, denial, repression, rationalization, delaying tactics, etc. Rationalization seems to increase internal distress and self-alienation, which in turn lead to the escalation of addictive behavior. A drug becomes a tranquilizer for the psychic distress that it causes.

"Neurological science has effectively demonstrated that mind is brain and brain is body." In the old Hebrew sense, the belief was that "human are beings who are souls, rather than bodies who have souls."

In order for the body to work in harmony, it is important to maintain the natural balance. A stress reaction is an example of what can result when the body's equilibrium is thrown off balance. If we are psychologically healthy, our systems should function in harmony and be easily interchangeable.

[2]Wegscheider-Cruse defines "co-dependency" as a pattern of painful dependency on compulsive behaviors and on approval from others in an attempt to find safety, self-worth, and identity. Recovery is possible."

" In co-dependency, it is the interaction between one's own manufactured *brain chemicals* (having to do with our reinforcement center) and one's behavior that stimulates the brain to establish compulsive and addictive behavior processes."

Wegscheider-Cruse calls the excessive rush produced by our brain that gets us into self-defeating behaviors and keeps that rush coming—"co-dependency."

The belief here is that change in the body chemistry that creates addictions is the result of having the disease of co-dependency and not the cause. Wegscheider-Cruse calls the disease "co-dependency." I call the disease *"primal deprivation.*" It can also be called "narcissistic injury" or "structural symbiotic toxicity."

"We know that we can become intoxicated and toxic with our own internal chemicals set off by behavior, and we can become addicts to and through our own behavior that can trigger certain chemicals that satisfy our craving for relief."

[3] "Mind/Body Medicine," *Alternative Medicine: The Definitive Guide.* Psychoneuroimmunology (PNI) is a rapidly expanding field. Studies of the immune system, which gave birth to PNI, helped in the clarification of the relationship between mind and body.

Science can now confirm that emotional fluctuations and status do have a direct influence upon whether a human organism will be well or get sick. Researchers can now say that intelligence is located in every cell of the body and that separation of the mind and body no longer applies. However, each person is unique and this condition is called "biochemical individuality" (Roger Williams, Ph.D.). Chronic stress and lack of chemical balance contribute to illness.

"The ability of a multiple personality patient to substitute personalities when in pain is an example of how mind/body medicine can accelerate the healing process."

[4] Carlton K. Erickson, Ph.D., "The Neurochemistry of Craving," *Treatment Today.* "A primary characteristic of dependence is impaired control over use of the drug."

There is a changing way of looking at addiction. At first, cocaine was thought to have no significant withdrawal symptoms (it was considered emotional rather than physical). So "lack of withdrawal" was used to prove that cocaine was not addictive.

Dependence, as we look at it today, has both psychological and physical characteristics. An obsessive preoccupation with drug use results in impaired control. Scientists now believe that the neurochemical dysfunction in addictions can best be described as a "chemical deficiency" (dopamine and serotonin). This chemical deficiency disease can be compared to diseases such as Parkinsonism (dopamine deficiency) and diabetes (lack of proper insulin release in the pancreas). What is revealed in new findings is that drug dependence is a disease over which the individual has no control. The process can be "best characterized as a brain chemistry-deficiency disease."

[5]Steven Levenkron, *Obsessive-Compulsive Disorders: Treating and Understanding Crippling Habits.* There are those who suffer from "obsessional disorders," which this author coins excessive "overthinking." "An obsessional disorder might be characterized not by symptoms or moods, but by particular behaviors to control anxiety and depression."

Eating disordered people have some of the same complaints those with obsessional disorders describe; for example: emptiness, moods, and limitations. OCD has been seen as a neurological defect (something wrong with the brain). The author states, "OCD is the personality's attempt to reduce anxiety, which may stem from a painful childhood or genetic tendency toward anxiety that just won't quit." OCD is a "pervasive condition that causes individuals to over-examine their thoughts, spoken words, actions, productivity, and relationships." The end result is that these individuals always assess themselves as inadequate and lacking. The repeated activities, or rituals, or self-soothing devices are used to "fill an emotional emptiness caused by under-parenting or impaired parenting in early childhood." Often this is the result of the parent figure being either missing, weakened, or depleted to the degree that a role reversal between parent and child occurred. "Repetition brings familiarity, and familiarity is the opposite of the unknown." Repetition breeds a sense of the predictable, and predictability is safe.

The belief is that the seeds of vulnerability toward OCD

are planted in the first four years of life—the years where the bonding between mother and child take place. Often these seeds precede birth with a disposition (heredity) to anxiety and/or depression. With these factors in place, the onset of OCD usually awaits some traumatic event before it begins to emerge.

Anorexia nervosa (behaviors conceived as identity) is a form of OCD. Malnutrition creates "an organic mind syndrome that enhances obsessionality." This is the most complex and seductive obsessional and obsessive-compulsive disorder. With bulimia-nervosa bingeing, vomiting, and laxatives become the hidden regulators of anxiety, panic, and depression. Chronic use (binge, purge) becomes a part of anxiety-depression regulation, and is incorporated as a defense mechanism with other obsessive-compulsive rituals. Obsessional disorders seem to correspond with being raised by parents who are needy themselves. I have come across those who get a release from cutting themselves. When the question is asked: What do you get out of cutting? The response is "Pain." Pain is described as bringing oneself back, back from being away from being away from away from oneself (dissociative state). Another response was either "relief" or a "rush!"

[6] *Biological Components of Substance Abuse and Addiction*, compiled by the U.S. Congress, Office of Technology Assessment. The brain reward system is affected by most drugs of abuse. When there is drug abuse, there is an interaction that takes place within the neurochemical mechanisms of the brain. Repeated use of all drugs of abuse is associated with neuroadaptive responses. "Certain aspects of withdrawal, such as changes in mood and motivation induced by the chronic drugged state, may be key factors to relapse and drug-seeking behaviors."

[7] Phillips. The word "container" has a particular usage in the theoretical system of the author. It is derived from

Donald Winnicott's "the maternal holding environment." "Containers" used in this context are the uterus, a mother's arms, the Ego, and the concentric environments of society and Nature. In other words, a holding, cuddling, nutrient environment—Mother Earth. For the native American, the circle is more than a symbol, it is the embodied template for containing and being contained." Phillips' concepts of the Person (human animal), the Ego and the Self, are seen as different from some traditional models.

Fetal physiology is greatly influenced by the emotional state of the mother during the pregnancy (which can be "episodic" or "fixed"). The developing fetus' history originates in utero and is influenced by "parental expectation, generational family patterns, and maternal physiology." Developmentalists propose that there are two mothers incorporated into Ego's experience: close-up "object-mother," and the non-visible "environmental mother." Effects of the environment will influence and shape the quality of life. "Unbalanced environments produce unbalanced families who raise unbalanced children."

CHAPTER V

"Mind is brain and brain is body."
Gerald May

Conclusion

Impact Of My Theory

At this time there are those who either believe in the medical model (disease theory) of addiction and others who believe in the psychological model (decision theory). Many insights have come into play that point to genetic theories and with all that is before us, there are those who would still argue the point. Again, we look at black and white thinking. When we talk about a decision, it indicates that we have a choice. When we talk about disease, it indicates that we don't have a choice until we are educated. I believe that my theory lies somewhere midstream at this point. I do not lean in either direction. I have supported both theories at different points in my career. Since I have stated which came first, the "chicken or the egg" and still question that, I find myself leaning toward the innate conditioning prior to birth and *primal deprivation* as the possible cause of energy shifts. This would eventually throw us out of balance and deplete what was a part of the natural flow. I hope that this knowledge will spark others or at least create enough doubt to open the channels of the great minds that I know are out there. I believe it could add new dimensions to the treatment field and erase part of the stigma that still exists. When we talk about alcoholism (addiction) as a disease, it removes a level of responsibility for the happening. With the focus on decision, it indicates that we have made a choice. It is interpreted as total responsibility. When we address alcohol problems and eating disorders, however, there is a different attitude among professionals toward the individual. There are very few who really look at the origin. Treatment recommendation toward a course of action can be directed in a more humane way. I hope that attitudes mature and that there are professionals who look at the individuals before them as complex beings as opposed to people about whom they can make simplistic judgments. There needs to be mandatory education for all those who treat addiction on any level. Professionals must be tuned in to all aspects of this complex and overwhelming problem. It is most difficult for both the individual and the provider to understand.

The main theory of my work evolves from *primal deprivation*. I deal with addictive behaviors from a holistic perspective of "body/mind." My goal has been to create enough insight and doubt among those of us who have an interest in this field. I also hope that it creates enough interest to challenge those interested with the energy to explore further. Speaking for society as a whole is a greater picture. Education is one aspect of opening the channels for improved treatment. There are so many flaws in the treatment of addictions because of limited knowledge and the fact that so few really know how to address it. I see enabling as a huge problem within the field. I mean here "enabling" in the sense of being party to the "visitors" to therapy, who have no desire for solution to their problems or have the expectation that the therapist, program, or group can fix them (an outside job). We are for the most part an "other-directed" population. Energies and teachings are geared to getting across the importance of being "inner-directed." Everything I say spells out the concept that the level of health or "unhealth" is generated from within each of us. The healing begins when we recognize that it is an "inside job" and that we have everything we need within us. I believe that as a society the process of healing with respect to looking at the subject at hand is a huge undertaking. The process has been evolving and movement has been happening. As professionals our problem is that as we look at the greater picture, we must be willing to expand our views and methods of practice. There are always those who stand rigid in what they think is working, and they are not willing to step out of the 12 x 12 square. Some of us are caught in the remnants of our own pathology, which limits our ability to risk where doubt (fear) emerges.

I want to encapsulate the following: 1) Transfer of Addictions; 2) Addictive Diseases and the Complex Symptoms of the Addictive Malaise; and 3) Alteration of the Energy System With Alternative Methods to Restore Balance.

1) Transfer Of Addiction: I believe that the Transfer of Addiction is negative movement usually unnoticed by the addict. It surfaces as an individual lets go of the preferred means used. It helps to recreate the familiar feeling with another source. There is often some hidden secondary gain that helps to keep denial going. Here the denial manifests itself as the need for the physiological and psychological familiar feelings of deprivation (empty), the adrenaline rush, and a sense of powerlessness, helplessness. This brings about the shame-based feelings and keeps them alive. When I think of moderation, I think of balance. Yet, when told that anything in moderation is positive, many people have no concept of what that means. In actuality it can be considered abstract in nature since we must agree that it relates to an individual perspective. Anything done in moderation is seen as healthy. It is when one exceeds moderation that it is considered abusive in nature. Whatever is overdone, whether it is drinking, attending Alcoholics Anonymous meetings, exercise, sex, etc., it can become a form of abuse. So often this progresses to a transfer of addictions or the way we treat the symptom as individuals instead of addressing the cause.

Complex Symptoms of Addictive Malaise:

"Malaise" is a vague sense of mental or moral ill-being. The symptoms that are common range from: 1) the adrenaline rush which creates that "on the edge" feeling; 2) feelings of deprivation (empty) that set up searching for any means of filling up and sometimes out; 3) dissociation, which can be considered the means by which one escapes from not dealing with whatever is at hand that may be overwhelming, traumatic, etc.; 4) a common phenomena is intimacy dysfunction—one of the aftermaths of the family system experience; 5) there is also boundary inadequacy, which is still another way to keep an abusive stance; 6) to be abuse-prone is a learned behavior which is environmental in nature; 7) what follows all of this is a sense of powerlessness; 8) and what surfaces when not into addictive styles is that shame-based core; 9) and the inability to choose to let go of this repetitive cycle.

Alteration of the Energy System With Alternative Methods to Restore Balance:

It is obvious that the body chemistry and its balance is affected by external and internal influences. With new programming, I propose that there is a solid chance to restore nature's balance. We have available to us so many alternative healing methods to explore. I have dealt with a few in this study, e.g. TFT, Guided Imagery, Relaxation Response, Affirmations to Baroque Music. The state of the mind affects the working of the system, the shifting of energy, and shifting the cellular makeup, which in turn alters the body and its performance. In addition to that, how one nourishes, exercises, and rests the body, plays a vital part in its performance, both physically and mentally. If one puts cheap gas into a car, after a while the car may not function well. If I have a diet that predominantly consists of refined sugars or alcohol, over time (depending on the individual) with abusive use, the body becomes dependent. This is because actual physiological shifts take place, altering the body/mind. Since mind is body and body is mind, or the fact that the human being is considered an energy field, then surely it can be said that we are body-mind with body in mind and mind in body. So the statement that everything affects everything else is crystal clear. In an effort to use or at least think in terms of a holistic view of the individual, I can truly claim that all of the different methodology I have used has worked. It has worked when the investment was clearly there and the individual was not locked into the pathology for whatever might be the secondary gain.

An Analogy

When we plant a seed in healthy, balanced soil, we get a healthy plant. When a seed is planted in soil that is unhealthy, we have all observed the poor results at one time or another. If the environment is one of balance and the plant is nourished in this environment, it thrives. However, if the external environment is toxic, the seed and then progressively, the plant suffers the consequences. So in terms of balance, there is balance whether it be a living plant or a living being. We can all safely say that what we think, feel, do, eat, drink, don't eat, will shift the balance of the energy system accordingly. One of my clients who has been in sobriety for twelve years stated, "I believe alcoholism is a dietary problem." This person believes that instead of the cause of alcoholism being a possible defective gene, that its cause is dietary. He also believes that he has choice. Given that statement, he said, "I have chosen not to get out of this cycle." This was in response to the recognition that he continues to transfer to other addictions.

Are We In Love With Addiction?

I have heard it said in many ways that "We are in love with our addiction." It is that special moment—the endless moment of a high, euphoria, or elation, that we chase. It truly is an exquisite moment, even though it that spirals down and is lost in a flash! One is often left with the ravages of shame—yet this becomes a repetition compulsion. I think of those who suffer from anorexia and bulimia and the references they make to that very special relationship they have with their "malaise." It surely has been a very close and special relationship. On some level, it is the master that symbolizes love. What about the alcoholic, with alcohol at the center? It has often been said, "alcohol is his mistress." So in essence addictions can be seen as "love affairs." How does one get out of this circle (maze)? I believe it is choice and faith that there is another way. For after all, when we reach in and realize that with a spiritual connection there is serenity that is so exquisite, for that is balance.

Summary

The desire to explore addictive behaviors on a deeper level, to bring into focus avenues toward a more holistic approach to treatment, and to develop a more conscious body-mind attitude was my purpose. I brought to the reader my theories involving body-mind with consideration drawn to both the internal and external environment. I gave suggestions on the influence on human energy and its outcomes. I have given countless examples of the seeds that planted my "discoveries." I have discussed body-mind, physical/mental changes, and transfer of addictions. The end result still points to the influence that the way one lives life, thinks, and acts contributes to the chemistry or the chemical makeup of the entire system. I have written a great deal and presented my views in different ways as a means of getting across what I believe are the valuable points of this study. The series of diagrams and continuums that have evolved have been my style of painting the picture of what I believe is happening in mind, body, and spirit to the individuals who are plagued by an energy produced over time. This energy evolves from the external environment, individual perception, reactions to those perceptions, the individual and/or familial design, or the creation of a Higher Power. My "paintings" are not scientific in nature. They were created from the few and the many, who through their processes painted the murals of the insights, hunches, intuitions of my interpretation of "body-mind." As human beings, we all have a set of basic needs for survival: 1) food and water; 2) safety and security; 3) love and affection; 4) self-esteem; and 5) self-actualization (Maslow, 1954). I believe that we can evolve to a level of self-actualization if we choose. In the Alcoholics Anonymous program, the belief is that there exists "an obsession of the mind and an allergy of the body." This is a true statement! All that I have written, I propose as *The Cause*! There is yet more to come. For if there is doubt within those who cast their eyes upon these words and pictures, it must be remembered that "doubt is the path to discovery," without which there might be a blank slate!

Beginnings

All beginnings are hard. You
cannot swallow the world at
one time. Be patient—all
beginnings are hard, especially
a beginning that you made by
yourself. That is the hardest
beginning of all. I marvel that
we survive our beginnings.

From *In the Beginning*,
Chaim Potak

Index

Q

qualitative addictions 97

R

receiving situations 30
receiving system 30, 31, 55
relapse 66
repetition compulsion 31, 71
"repetition compulsion" 90
Roberts, Denton 37, 43, 45, 59, 68
role reversal 61, 71, 98
rush 63

S

sabotage 67
script analysis 31
Secondary Un-Natural Symbiosis 55
self-flagellation 51
self-indulging 51
self-kindness 52
self-talk 45, 48, 52
Self-Talk/Abuse 52
self-will-run-riot 53
serotonin 112
sex addiction 78
Sexton, Dan 59
sexual addiction 33
sexual demon 39
sexual trauma 39
SOAR 31, 42, 59, 75, 88, 93
spiritual health 70
Steiner, Claude, Ph.D. 31
stress 61
stressor 67
structural symbiotic systems 29, 31, 103
"surrender" 85
symbiosis 29, 55
symbiotic relational system 30
symbiotic systems 57

T

The Lineup 83

The Search 91
theme-of-life 31
Thought Field Therapy 32, 34, 35, 58, 72, 81, 96, 106, 108
Tom 108
toxic shame 32
tranquilizer 58, 96
Transactional Analysis 27, 54, 116
Transactional Analysis model 29
Transfer Of Addiction 126
Transfer of Addictions 66
True Self System 91, 113
"tunnel vision" 101
Twelve-Step programs 53

U

unbalanced family system 113
unhealthy core beliefs 51
unhealthy symbiosis 55
Urge Reduction 32, 35, 72, 109

W

willpower 53
"workaholism" 33